HISTORICAL PARADORS

Acknowledgements

The society of Spanish hotels (Paradores de Turismo de España) has been an invaluable help for the production of this edition.

Original edition © Lunwerg Editores, Barcelona, 1997
Text © 1997 Juan Eslava Galán
Photos © 1997 Francisco Ontañón
Original title: Paradores históricos

Copyright © 1999 for the English text.
Könemann Verlagsgesellschaft mbH
Bonner Str. 126, D-50968 Cologne

Translation from Spanish: Richard Rees and Lucilla Watson

ISBN 84-7782-606-4
Depósito legal: B-13536-2002

LUNWERG EDITORES
Beethoven, 12 - 08021 BARCELONA - Tel. 93 201 59 33 - Fax 93 201 15 87
Sagasta, 27 - 28004 MADRID - Tel. 91 593 00 58 - Fax 91 593 00 70

Printed in Spain

HISTORICAL PARADORS

A JOURNEY THROUGH SPANISH HOTELS

LUNWERG
EDITORES, S.A.

Arab fortresses, old monasteries, palaces, medieval castles... Unique buildings of yesterday, recovered today so that travellers may find accommodation within ancient, noble walls, where the shadows of the past still preserve imperishable memories, engraved on the stone, the adobe, the wood, on stairways and passages, in dining rooms and salons; where sculptures, paintings, and architecture speak of our history.

These are the Paradors of Spain. Magic hotels that harmoniously combine the legacy of the past with high-quality modern service. Places in which to enjoy all the variety of landscapes, of traditional cuisine with the finest produce, and the history of buildings and a country characterised by nuances and contrasts.

And all this thanks to a network of establishments that dates back to 1928, when H.M. Alphonso XIII inaugurated the first Parador.

TABLE OF CONTENTS

HISTORICAL PARADORS
A JOURNEY THROUGH SPANISH HOTELS

It was April, the season when snow melts on the high peaks and full, swift-flowing rivers run to the sea through shady woods and sunny meadows. The traveler, who all winter long had dreamed of the castles and other magical places of Spain, packed his baggage and crossed the Pyrenees by the high mountain pass of Bentarte, in the Basque country.

Now in his middle years, the traveler had already journeyed to many places and explored the remote landscapes of distant countries. He had spent the long winter evenings preparing his journey; he had planned his route, well aware that the roads that he was to follow had been wearily and fearfully trodden by many equally curious wayfarers long before him. In 3000 years of history, countless visitors had explored the remote western peninsula of Europe, the land where the Greeks dreamed of the Garden of the Hesperides, the gray and green clifftops from which the Romans watched the sun sink into the ocean depths of Finisterre (*Finis Terrae*), the world's end.

Humming an old song, the traveler imagined that, 1000 years before him, the mountains and woods that watched him go by had also witnessed the passage of Johan de Gorz, the ambassador whom Otto I of Germany had sent to the mighty caliph of Córdoba. He reflected how, not long afterward, those meadows and peaks were the traveling companions of a refined throng of romantics – Washington Irving, Ford Madox Ford, Théophile Gautier, George Borrow, Prosper Mérimée – and other anonymous visitors who came in search of the picturesque and Oriental exoticism of the legendary cities of the south. He also resolved to reach, unhurriedly and in easy stages, the dream cities of the Iberian peninsula: Burgos and Santiago, Toledo and Ronda, Málaga and Granada, Córdoba and Seville, Cadiz and the coastline of southern Spain.

The traveler, a dreamer who carried the whole of European history in his mental baggage, decided to begin his itinerary through Spain from the north; he would follow the highways of European monastic culture which, carried in the backpacks of pilgrims down the road to Santiago, met and melded with Oriental culture, a stream of influence flowing in the opposite direction along the ancient Roman roads that saw the onrush of the African hordes when the sultans of Marrakech swore to water their horses in the Tiber, that is, in the heart of Europe.

Crossing the Pyrenees, and contemplating the craggy, tree-covered slopes, the traveler believed for a moment that in the perfect silence of the morning he had heard the harsh tones of Roland's hunting horn; the hero of French legend perished here in the 8th century, along with the whole of Charlemagne's rearguard, at the hands of the indomitable Basques. As he negotiated the rugged roads of the cordillera, the traveler started thinking about the peculiar history of the land that stretched out before him. This isolated corner of Europe attracted Phoenicians and Greeks, who came in search of mineral ores; the Romans made of it a prosperous province that provided their empire not only with silver and olive oil but also with emperors and warriors, poets and philosophers. During the dark Middle Ages it was peopled by Nordic tribes: Suevians, Alani, and finally Visigoths, who founded a kingdom in Toledo. In 711 it was conquered by the Moors and that same year the Christians, who had sought refuge in the mountains of northern Spain, began the slow, laborious task of reconquest that continued for eight centuries, ending in 1492. During that long epoch, a rich, variegated, and contradictory society flourished, an alloy forged from cultures as different and yet as complementary as the Christian, the Moslem, and the Jewish. The Iberian peninsula was, and in the deepest recesses of its culture continues to be, simultaneously Spain, Al-Andalus and Sepharad.

In 1492 the Catholic Kings – Isabella of Castile and Ferdinand of Aragon – conquered the Moslem kingdom of Granada and sent Columbus to discover America. With their successors, the Habsburgs, Spain became the empire "on which the sun never set," but the gold and silver that the bulging galleons brought back from the Americas were squandered on countless wars in Europe, Africa, and the Mediterranean. Sudden prosperity was followed by slow decline peppered with civil wars that continued into the 19th century and even through to the 20th.

On that bright April morning, filled with anticipation as he passed through the shady forests of the Pyrenees, our traveler arrived in Spain.

HONDARRIBIA

The traveler was to spend his first night in Spain in the castle at Hondarribia, on the border with France, beside the babbling little Bidasoa river. This castle was built in the 10th century by Sancho Abarca, king of Navarre. At that time some half-dozen Christian kingdoms had tenuously established themselves in northern Spain, where they dwelt in a state of constant anxiety, paying taxes to the mighty caliphate of Córdoba or

Right: an interior view of the Parador Nacional El Emperador in Hondarribia. The sympathetic modern conversion preserves many of the original features of this 10th-century castle.

Below: the Parador Nacional El Emperador, in Hondarribia, Guipúzcoa.

HONDARRIBIA

The parador is housed in a castle built by Sancho Abarca, king of Navarre, in the 10th century and remodeled in the 16th century by the Emperor Charles V. The castle has provided lodgings for many great figures in European history, among them Joanna the Mad, Charles V, Philip III and Philip IV, and General Spínola, whose most famous victory for Spain was at the Surrender of Breda.

Due to its frontier location, the castle of Hondarribia played a crucial role in the wars between Spain and France. It was besieged successively by Francis I, by Cardinal Richelieu in 1638, and by Napoleon, under whose control it was from 1808 to 1813. The fortress also played host to important people in peacetime, notably many Spanish princesses on their way to France to marry French kings: Eleanor of Austria, wife of Francis I, Anne of Austria, wife of Louis XIII, and María Theresa of Austria, wife of Louis XIV, all stayed here.

falling victim to Moorish pillaging expeditions. However, the notorious Yacub al-Mansur, the invincible caliph who had sacked Santiago de Compostela and Barcelona, spared the kingdom of Sancho Abarca; this was because, placing greater trust in love than in the walls and turrets of Hondarribia, this Navarrese monarch had given al-Mansur one of his daughters in marriage.

Before entering his lodgings, the traveler paused to take in the fine austere façade of the parador, built by the Emperor Charles V. It was almost devoid of windows, and in the ancient ashlars he clearly

Standards emblazoned with lions and castles hark back to the past.

distinguished the pockmarks caused by ancient cannon-fire, which the 9-foot-thick castle walls had rebuffed with ease. At dusk he went out onto the terrace to watch the sun set over Txingundi Bay; there at his feet was the port, where the waters of the Bidasoa flow into the sea.

In Hondarribia there are even more ghosts – of great historical figures – than there are hostelries. The town provided lodgings for a host of Spanish or foreign princesses and queens on their way to and from France and the rest of Europe. Among them was Joanna the Mad, who lost her reason through jealousy of her husband, Philip the Fair; and also Isabelle of Valois, Isabel de Borbón, Isabel de Austria, Anne of Austria, and María Theresa of Austria. The ubiquitous appelation "of Austria" demonstrates the degree of intermarriage that took place for reasons of state; this led to inbreeding, which in turn caused the progressive degeneration of the royal lineage until the last of the Habsburgs sadly came into the world: this was the deformed imbecile Charles II the Bewitched.

During periods of relative peace, which occurred whenever the political climate allowed, Hondarribia still proudly maintained its warlike character. Although it succumbed briefly to the onslaught of Francis I of France, it was soon recaptured by the commander Iñigo Fernández de Velasco. In 1638, the town was besieged once again, but resolutely held out until reinforcements arrived and finally managed to break through; the event is commemorated each year by a military parade.

The walls of the parador are decorated with halberds, shields, and weavings.

Every room is imbued with a rich historical atmosphere.

The castle at Hondarribia overlooks the Bidasoa river. Here, where the river flows into the sea and vessels sail peacefully by, the turbulent history of this area can be relegated to the past.

OLITE

he following day, the traveler rose with the dawn. He planned to cross the plain of Vitoria, shrouded in downy mist in the early morning. Though not superstitious, he would have been delighted to run into a *baxajaun*, the name given hereabouts to those little elfish characters who occasionally emerge from the underworld to come to the aid of us mortals, or else to play practical jokes. According to Basque folklore, it was a *baxajaun* who taught the local inhabitants how to grow wheat, and for this favor he now appears as San Martinico on church altars.

Rounding a bend in the road, the traveler suddenly found himself face to face with the Gothic castle of Olite. Lulled into a dream on his passage through ancient woods and fresh meadows, he fancied that what he saw must be a mirage. Could this be the castle of the Nibelungen? Or a château of the Loire? Or another palace built for the popes of Avignon? The castle of Olite, its towers crowned by glistening black-slated pinnacles, with mullioned windows and brilliant stained glass, seemed to the traveler to be more like a heavenly vision than something of this earth.

Around 620, at the time of its foundation, Olite was the stronghold of the Visigothic king Suintila. Later it was the fortified palace of the kings of Navarre. It reached the apogee of its splendor under Charles II the Noble, a king "endowed with wisdom, temperance and virtues," and a keen botanist who planted his orchards and gardens with jasmines from Alexandria, grapefruit trees, citrons, and other exotic plants never before seen in Europe. After this period of courtly magnificence there came decline, although the embers of the brilliance that marked the reign of Charles II still glowed for his grandson, the prince of Viana, who kept wild beasts and exotic fowl in the castle courtyards.

OLITE

The castle at Olite is an imposing fortified Gothic palace, much influenced by the French style. The slate roofs of its round towers contrast vividly with the austere brown ashlars of its walls. The original 13th-century fortress was remodeled in the 15th century. The whole building was destroyed by fire in the 18th century, but has now been restored and converted into a parador.

The traveler took a stroll in the medieval town that clustered around the fortress. He greatly admired the Gothic altarpiece in the church of Santa María, the town walls, and the Rúa Mayor, along which so many pilgrims had trudged on their way to Santiago de Compostela. He also had time to visit the mysterious sanctuary of Eunate, to which people from many foreign lands made devout pilgrimages before the spread of Christianity. According to scholars, it was because of the popularity of this shrine that the Knights Templar built a strange octagonal church on this very spot in the middle of the fields.

Right: *the interior of the parador.*
Previous page: *the castle at Olite, now converted into a parador.*

"No king has either a palace or a castle as beautiful as this, nor a greater number of gilded rooms," wrote a 15th-century traveler.

Two views of Olite: the 13th-century royal palace (above) and (right) the Gothic façade of the church of Santa María, which dates from the second half of the 13th century.

LEÓN

Rejoining the pilgrimage route to Santiago, the traveler reached Nájera, where lie the tombs of the ancient kings of Navarre.

"I must correct you: Nájera never formed part of the kingdom of Navarre. It was a kingdom in itself; because, when Sancho Garcés conquered the valley of the Ebro as far as Tudela, what he created was the kingdom of Nájera."

The traveler, who was not about to argue over one kingdom more or less, accepted the local scholar's reprimand and continued on his way to visit the monasteries of Suso and Yuso, in San Millán de la Cogolla, the birthplace of the Spanish language. Then, following the road that marks the course of long stretches of the ancient pilgrimage route, he crossed the plain where stands Santo Domingo de la Calzada; in this famous cathedral there is a Gothic-style hencoop, carved in stone with an artistically wrought grille, in which a cockerel and a hen live happily together. The traveler had already heard a riddle, which goes like this:

Santo Domingo de la Calzada
do cantó la gallina después de asada.

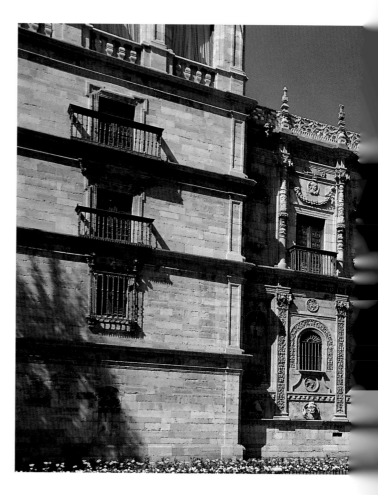

LEÓN

The Casa Primada de la Orden de Caballeros de Santiago was founded in 1152. A church and a hostelry were later added to serve the needs of the pilgrims on their way to and from Santiago. The present building dates from the early 16th century and features the work of such artists as Juan de Badajoz, Juan de Juni, Pedro de Ibarra, and Guillermo Doncel. It has a remarkable Plateresque façade; the building's other ornamental details are fully Baroque. The cloister, now a museum, contains panels, paintings, and sculptures spanning the 10th to the 17th centuries.

(Santo Domingo de la Calzada
Where the chicken crowed after it was roasted)

The rhyme alludes to a legend that was already part of local folklore when the Lord of Caumont came to these lands in 1417.

The story goes that a family of pilgrims were staying at a local inn, where one of the serving wenches took a fancy to a young man who had come with them. Receiving no response to her coquetry, she became so enraged that she vowed to cause his downfall. To this end, she hid a valuable chalice among her unfortunate victim's belongings and waited until the family had proceeded on their way before denouncing the theft and blaming the youth. The merciless local judge sentenced the presumed thief to death by hanging and, having passed sentence, His Honour returned to the inn with the kind of ravenous appetite that the administration of justice inevitably brings. While he was waiting for his roast chicken to be served, people came from the village to tell him that the condemned man was still alive, even though they had hanged him with a brand new rope. It seemed that an angel or some other supernatural force had held him in the air to prevent his dying.

– "Do you mean to tell me you've hanged him and he's still alive?" asked the incredulous judge.

– "Yes, Your Honour. Although we hanged him over an hour ago he's still alive and well. The rope is a good one and his feet are three spans above the ground. There's no mistake."

– "Impossible. If what you say is true, that man is as alive as this chicken," said the judge, preparing to sink his teeth into the roast fowl that the innkeeper had just placed before him.

Just then, as if by divine intervention, the roast chicken rose up in its platter and let out a resounding cock-a-doodle-doo. The terrified judge ordered the young man to be brought down from the gallows, and spared his life.

The traveler, who had heard so much praise heaped upon the *pulchra leonina* – the Leónese beauty, as León Cathedral was known in the days when Latin was the European lingua franca – was impatient to see its imposing stained-glass windows. Taking a road that led him through woodlands and green cultivated fields, he aimed to reach León before sundown.

Above: *the parador's Renaissance cloister.*

Right: *one of the public rooms of the parador.*

Previous page: *the Parador de León, formerly the monastery of San Marcos, which was begun in 1531 by Juan de Badajoz.*

Two views of the parador: above, looking into the cloister from the interior and, right, the cloister. The vaulting of the Renaissance cloister is also by Juan de Badajoz, while some of the statues of apostles and saints that adorn the monastery are attributed to Juan de Juni.

León stands at a crossroads and such is its position of strategic importance that the Romans established the garrison for their seventh legion here; the city's name is derived from *legio*, the Latin word for legion, and remains of the garrison can still be seen in the vestiges of its ancient walls. It was here also that the Alfonso I, king of Asturias, established his stronghold as a defense against the Moors. The illustrious city was later to be the capital of a kingdom which, as a traditional saying states, *Tuvo veinticuatro reyes/antes que Castilla leyes* ("had 24 kings before Castile even had laws"), and that was one of the major landmarks encountered on the pilgrimage route to Santiago. This serendipitous situation put the people of León in contact with European culture – and European culture in contact with the people of León.

Making his way to the parador, the visitor crossed the Bernesga river and thought about the quantity of water that must have flowed beneath the eroded voussoirs of that stone bridge since Edward Cook Widdrington, the English traveler who explored León in 1829, wrote: "There can be no beauty comparable to the arabesques and adornments of the façade of [the monastery of] San Marcos." As he admired the stonework that decorates this impressive building, the traveler, who had recently read Cavafy, was seized by the almost unbearable sense of joy that on very rare occasions results from coming face to face with beauty. Then, quickening his step, he entered the parador.

The parador of León originates from a hostelry for pilgrims founded in the 12th century by a local princess, the Infanta Doña Sancha, "as lodging for the poor people of Christ." The original building was later remodeled to become the seat of the Military Order of Santiago (one of the local orders of soldier friars established in Spain at the time of the Crusades, to fight against the Moors). The new building, now the monastery of San Marcos, was designed in the Plateresque style, a transitional style midway between Gothic and Spanish Renaissance that imitates the meticulous craft of silversmiths (plateros), the artisans who produced sumptuous silver services for the nobility. The monastery later became a school, a civilian prison, a church prison, a barracks – and a stud farm. In one of its gloomy dungeons, "with a stream for a bedhead," Francisco de Quevedo, the famous poet and novelist of the Spanish Golden Age, languished for almost four years. Having walked round the cloister, the courtyards, and the rooms of the parador, which were furnished with antiques, the traveler visited its museum; here he saw a Romanesque ivory figure of Christ, one of the finest in Europe, and other remarkable Romanesque and Gothic sculptures. This fascinating display engrossed him until lunchtime. Then, he hungrily ate a substantial local stew, its distinctive flavor produced by eight contrasting varieties of meat: beef, chicken, pig's ear, dried

meat, black pudding, pork shoulder, bacon and *chorizo* (spiced pork sausage).

After a siesta, he stepped out into the city to visit the Collegiate Church of San Isidoro; here is displayed the royal pantheon of the former kings of León beneath a vault painted with charming Romanesque frescoes. The vision of their beauty still in his mind's eye, the traveler spent the rest of the afternoon wandering the streets of the medieval city, stopping to admire ancient palaces and ancestral homes emblazoned with coats of arms. In those narrow, twisting streets once lived the *omes buenos* (wise men), who in 1188, during the reign of Alfonso IX, constituted the first parliament in Europe.

That night the traveler slept a deep and peaceful sleep in his high canopied bed, lulled by the croaking of frogs in the nearby river. The following morning he returned to the pilgrimage route to Compostela.

The choir of León Cathedral, with its intricately carved stalls.

Exterior view of León Cathedral,
one of the most important examples
of Spanish Gothic architecture.

Not far from León, beside the Orbigo river, he stopped so as to enjoy the pleasure of crossing by the old footbridge and feeling beneath his feet the ancient stones worn smooth by the passage of minstrels, ladies, knights, beggars, saints, and bandits over centuries of pilgrimage. Halfway over the bridge, he stopped to read an inscription on a votive column: "The knight Suero de Quiñones, to free himself from the thrall in which his lady held him, and in pursuit of lasting fame, agreed with nine fellow knights to defend the pass beside this bridge by breaking lances against over 70 knights who came to the pilgrimage route of the Apostle Santiago from Castile, Aragon, Catalonia, Valencia, Portugal, Britain, Italy, and Germany." Don Suero broke as many lances in tournaments as he challenged European knights who dared joust with him as a token of his passion and to prove his love.

Santiago de Compostela

Crossing Galicia, by day following the trajectory of the sun, by night that of the Milky Way, the pilgrim proceeded toward Finisterre, the end of the earth (*finis terrae*) where the sea merges into the dark ocean beyond which, in the imagination of the people of the Middle Ages, lurked monsters and evil portents. It was early morning as the traveler journeyed in a landscape of soft meadows and thickly wooded groves covered in mist; he felt his pulse quicken as he recalled the fact that over nine centuries devout "Franks, Gascons, Bretons, Burgundians, Provençals, Normans, English, Germans, Lombards, and people from other nations and cultures beside" had ploughed the seas and crossed the rivers and mountains of Europe, undaunted by severe winters and scorching summers, epidemics and highwaymen, to make the pilgrimage to the tomb of St James the Apostle, known in Spanish as Santiago.

With these thoughts in mind, the traveler reached the Lavacolla river, the last stage of the journey before he climbed the hill from which the black towers and red roofs of Santiago may be contemplated. It was the custom for pilgrims to wash their shoes in the hospitable waters of the Lavacolla before appearing before the Apostle. It was equally customary for those who carried a change of clothes to burn their foul-smelling, threadbare traveling attire and present themselves before him cleanly dressed.

If in Europe there are half a dozen cities worthy of the name, cities with their own distinctive soul and that are more than mere agglomerations of buildings, then Santiago is certainly one of these. The pilgrim entered Santiago with his heart beating like that of a captive bird. A fine shower of rain, known locally as *orvallo*, was falling, refreshing meadows and gardens,

The Hospital de los Reyes Católicos, (previous page) *was founded in 1499 as a hostelry for pilgrims. As a parador* (above) *it is still an ideal stopping place for travelers.*

but it was quickly followed by a radiant morning sun shining through the clouds. This the pilgrim took as a sign of the Apostle's welcome.

Crossing the old city, and walking between ancient buildings with pretty wooden balconies and stonework covered in moss and verdigris, the traveler came to an enormous stone plaza known as the Obradoiro (from the verb *obrar,* to labor). It was here that masons dressed the stone for the buildings that enclose the plaza: these are the cathedral and the Hospital de los Reyes Católicos (now a parador), the Raxoy Palace, and the monastery of San Jerónimo.

The parador of Santiago, where the traveler had reserved a room, has a long, plain, sober façade that contrasts with its intricate Plateresque entrance. Its foundation document, dated 1499, proves that it is the world's oldest hotel, since the Catholic Kings built it "as a hostelry for pilgrims and to house

comfortably and suitably all devout people, both sick and in good health, who come to the city."

He was given a room, and having left his luggage there, the traveler took a stroll through the building; he admired its four courtyards, its coffered ceilings, its fountains, its stained-glass windows, and its sculptures and carpets, all sumptuous manifestations of the art of craftsmen of the past.

During this time the cathedral bells began to toll, summoning pilgrims; obeying their call, he crossed the square and climbed the Baroque staircase that leads to the basilica.

Santiago Cathedral has two façades, one behind the other, the outer façade acting as a protective screen for the inner. Looking at the outer façade, which is in the Baroque style, with intricate filigree decoration, no one would ever guess that it conceals a second, Romanesque façade, the finest of any

SANTIAGO DE COMPOSTELA

The former hostelry for pilgrims was built under the patronage of the Catholic Kings, by Enrique Egas and Diego de Muros. The central doorway is the work of Martín de Blas and Guillén Colás, and the façade was remodeled in 1678 under the supervision of Friar Tomás Alonso. The building faces onto the extensive Plaza del Obradoiro, bounded on its other three sides by the cathedral, the Palacio Raxoy, and the monastery of San Jerónimo.

The ornate Plateresque decoration of the parador's façade does not preclude a touch of modernity within.

Above and right: *two views within the parador, the former hostelry for pilgrims built under the patronage of the Catholic Kings.*

European cathedral. The pilgrim reflected that, if ever stones dressed by man were designed to sing the praises of the Creator, then these more than fulfilled their function. It might also be said that the work of quarrymen and masons continue to praise the Lord in the perfection of carved stone.

The traveler, who not only appreciated beauty and learning but also espoused the old adage that "When in Rome, do as the Romans do," joined the queue of devotees waiting to touch the head of a statue of the Spanish master Mateo, the man to whom is attributed that remarkable façade. Within the cathedral, he stood fascinated before the Botafumeiro, the largest censer in the world; standing as tall as a man, it is activated by eight sturdy friars and, swinging from side to side of the huge central aisle, gives off clouds of healthful smoke. This

Above: sunlight through the stained-glass windows of Santiago Cathedral.

Right: the ceiling of Santiago Cathedral.

remarkable device was first used in the 15th century to mask the stench of the multitudes, whose fervor was greater than their personal hygiene and who crowded into the cathedral on the major religious feast days. The Botafumeiro is still used today, though of course more for the sake of tradition than out of necessity.

Mingling with the crowd of devotees and occasionally allowing himself to be swept along by it, the traveler walked up and down the nave and the broad aisles of the cathedral. He climbed a narrow staircase behind the altar, and reached the statue of

The towers of the cathedral of Santiago de Compostela rising over the rooftops of the city.

Santiago, which he embraced, according to custom and ritual.

Now outside the cathedral again, the pilgrim began to walk round it, passing in turn in front of the façade of Las Platerías, the Puerta Real – the finest example of the Baroque style in Compostela – and the façade of La Azabachería, where he stopped at one of the stalls that nestle under the ancient walls to buy an amulet in the form of a pointing hand carved from deep black jet. Then the wanderer sought advice from an aged priest who, one step at a time, was slowly crossing the flagstones.

"Excuse me, father, where can I get a good meal hereabouts without being fleeced?"

The priest gazed at the traveler with amused irony.

"You can eat well anywhere in Compostela, but you'll enjoy the restaurant about halfway down that street over there."

"Thanks, and may God be with you."

In Compostela, tourists restore their energies with boiled and seasoned octopus, or scallops, which are the symbol of the pilgrim. With this they drink white Ribeiro or Albariño wines from a traditional white china cup. Our traveler could not resist the revered wine of the country, but instead of octopus or scallops he chose a Galician dish with an equally strong tradition: lampreys – cruel, mysterious fish with a meaty taste – stewed in their own juice. Truly, our traveler found, there is nothing like beauty to whet one's appetite.

Detail of the Pórtico de la Gloria, in the inner, Romaneque façade of the cathedral of Santiago de Compostela.

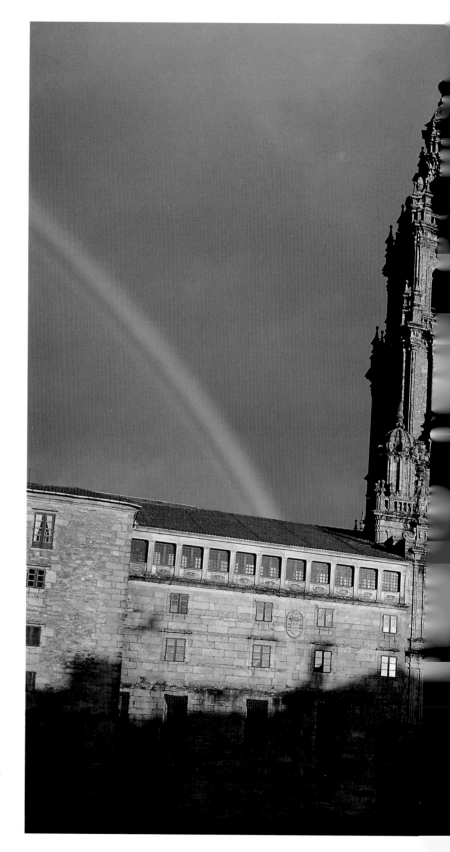

The main façade of the Obradoiro, one of the finest examples of Galician Baroque architecture.

VILLALBA

As he made his way along the roads of Galicia, a land of moss and granite, passing ancient palaces and *hórreos* (raised timber granaries), *cruceiros* (tall stone crosses) and houses with slate roofs, the traveler was willing to believe in old tales of hidden treasure guarded by a black dwarf; he felt at ease and once more began to daydream.

In Villalba clumps of trees rise taller than the hills and, in their colorful displays, market gardens rival the ever-flourishing meadows.

Right: *houses in Villalba, with their gray, slate-tiled roofs.*

Below: *the keep is, unusually, built on an octagonal ground plan. It is one of the most interesting medieval keeps in Galicia.*

In Villalba the traveler renewed his acquaintance with a good friend. "Villalba capon ... all the local countryside aromas pervade its grease, its flesh fattened on rye flour and mashed chestnuts. All the aromas of the firewood that burned for weeks on end beside the wicker *capoeiras* [hencoops] in country kitchens..." Now the traveler was conjuring up the words of the great Álvaro Cunqueiro. That morning he had crossed the rolling green carpet of the flatlands and, on reaching the Ladra river, had glimpsed between copses the battlements of the octagonal keep of the Andrade family castle; this was his destination and his lodging.

The keep of the old Andrade castle is massive, octagonal and almost windowless, but its austere and

VILLALBA

The keep, built by the Andrade family, stands in the city center, dominating a green, luxuriant landscape; it has about it an air of peaceful serenity that is far removed from the warlike events that were the reason for its existence. It is one of the most interesting medieval fortifications in Galicia; unusually for buildings of the period, it has an octagonal ground plan. The keep has now been converted into a parador. Access is by means of a drawbridge. It leads into the main drawing room, which is decorated with paintings of the successive lords of Andrade, "counts of Villalba," the family coat of arms and the insignia of the house of Andrade, the bear and the wild boar. There is also a stone sculpture of the boar on the tower's outer façade.

This unusual parador has a restaurant on the ground floor and six fine period-decorated rooms on the floors above. The keep is crowned by battlements commanding a view of the broad Terra Cha plateau.

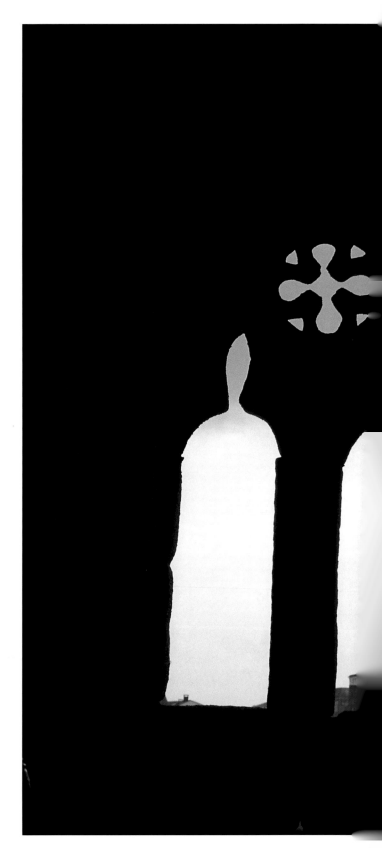

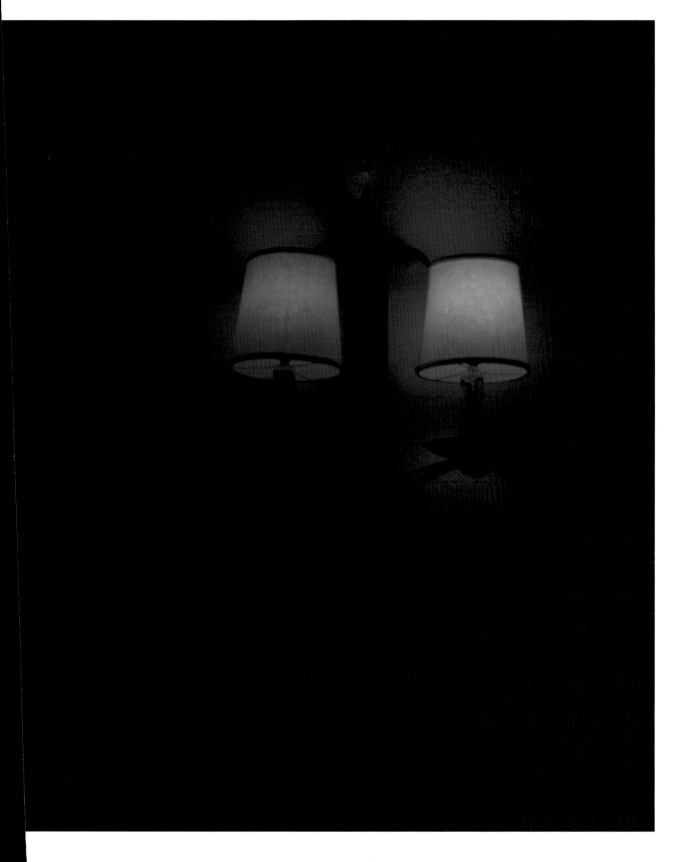

warlike appearance is relieved by the dark elongated shapes of cypress growing nearby and the luxuriant creeper that clings to it. This fortress was granted by Pedro the Cruel to Fernán Pérez de Andrade, the belligerent lord of vast territories in the region that stretch to the sea.

Having passed a granite *cruceiro*, the traveler stepped onto the drawbridge with that twinge of anxiety felt by everyone who crosses a drawbridge, however robust its timbers may be.

"The *cruceiro* that stands on a road to nowhere," they told him, "for at the foot of this tower perished many *irmandiños*, the medieval revolutionaries who led that famous uprising, the first revolution in Europe."

"And what were they demanding?"

"What did they want? What all revolutionaries want: a free supply of food from their lord's granary and the right to lift his lady's underskirts."

"And what did the Andrades do?"

"What anybody would do. When they were tired of cutting throats they put the *irmandiños* that were left to work on rebuilding the tower. That was around 1480, and the Andrades carried on levying taxes."

The traveler imagined that the Andrades, weaned on the capons paid to them in tribute, would have been a healthy, robust family, people capable of straightening a horseshoe with their bare hands or swimming across the lake after a night of passion.

Although he was more inclined to enjoy life's pleasures than dwell on the melancholy recollection of the dead, on his itinerary the traveler visited two tombs in the Gothic church of San Francisco de Betanzos: that of Cunqueiro in Mondoñedo, whose ambition to become archbishop of Manila was never realized, and that of Fernán Pérez de Andrade. Then the traveler strolled around the Betanzos estuary, an area of deep waters, black slate roofs, and green meadows.

Opposite page: *two views of the interior of the Parador Condes de Villalba.*

Above: *Villalba is set in unspoilt countryside.*

PONTEVEDRA

As he climbed the carpeted stone staircase, the traveler thought of all the hands that, over several generations, had added to the patina of the carved banisters: fine, gloved hands; white hands; chubby hands; rough hands; hands of ladies; of gentlemen; of yokels; hands made for milking and other satisfying tasks. The Casa del Barón, the palace that was to be the traveler's lodgings in Pontevedra, was built in the 16th century on the site of a Roman town house. In the 18th century it was extended by the Spanish grandee Don Benito de Lanzós, duke of Maceda, who added the tower and the spacious loggia, with its granite columns. The palace then passed into the ownership of the marquis of Figueroa and La Atalaya. The traveler imagined the marquis in his tight-fitting general's uniform at the foot of the staircase, turning round to look at his wife for the last time. Dressed in her long, blue silk Roman-style tunic, like those ladies in paintings by Goya, she bade him farewell from the gallery above the arch, with a wave of her snow-white hand (another hand for the banisters) and held back her tears. Only a few days later, shortly after midday on 14 July 1808, on a field scorched by gunpowder and blazing summer heat, the marquis was run through by a French lancer at the Battle of Medina de Rioseco.

After the death of the marquis, the building rapidly fell into decay. Soon after, the palace became a school for poor children and in the rooms that once were filled with the strains of the clavichord, skillfully played by the marchioness, the voices of young children could be heard in chorus reciting the Catechism. Later the building was used as a salt warehouse that supplied the tinned-food industry, and then it became a Masonic lodge, one of the many picturesque provincial charitable Masonic lodges that proliferated in 19th-century Spain, especially in such

The Casa del Barón, now the Parador de Pontevedra.

forward-looking maritime cities as Pontevedra. The palace reached its lowest ebb when its great rooms and corridors were partitioned into a warren of rooms; now it was a crowded tenement and the shabby furnishings brought in by its new occupiers contrasted with the solid vestiges of its former grandeur. It was saved from a dark fate at the hands of speculators and workmen wielding pickaxes by Don Eduardo de Vera y Navarro, Baron Goda; he purged the building of all trappings of degradation – the partition walls, the windows, and the roofs that had provided a few miserable dwellings – and restored to the building the palatial splendor

After suffering much neglect since the 16th century, the Parador de Pontevedra has been restored to its former palatial elegance.

PONTEVEDRA

The Pazo de Maceda was built on the foundations of a Roman villa. It was rebuilt in the 16th century, and extended in the 18th by the counts of Maceda, who made of it a typical pazo (Galician ancestral home). The original features of the building have been retained as much as possible. Both the façade and the main door are in the Neoclassical style. Outstanding interior elements are the original carved stone staircase and the old, typically Galician kitchen.

The most recent owner of the house was Baron Casa Goda, hence the parador's name: Casa del Barón.

with which it is once again endowed today.

Around midday, the traveler went out to stroll through the city, and quickly lost his sense of direction in the narrow streets around the harbor. It was a fine, sunny day and through the geraniums on the sill of an open window he saw lengths of dried octopus airing beside a stove. This was encouragement enough to inquire for an inn. In a tiny square he was torn between three temples of gluttony and gastronomy, finally allowing himself to be drawn in by one advertising seafood *filloa* in sea-urchin sauce, an original and subtle dish for connoisseurs of the road and the sea. Indeed, he was doubly fortunate for the establishment lacked the blaring television set that plagues this nation's humbler eating places and spoils the enjoyment of customers who want to eat in peace and quiet. After his feast the traveler, still savoring the flavor of the dark sea that suffused the urchins, returned to the

A cosy, welcoming room in the parador, with the staircase reflected in the ornate mirror.

Previous pages: *the cemetery overlooking the Miñor River in Pontevedra.*

Santa María la Mayor, in Pontevedra, a prime example of the Mudéjar style.

The church of the Virgen Peregrina, patron of Villalba.

parador, where he took a short siesta. He dreamed of the intricate paths followed by Teucer, the hero of Homeric legend, the mythical founder of Pontevedra when the port was called Helenes, before the Romans changed its name to Duos Pontes and later the Christians to Pontis Veteris. That afternoon the traveler wandered the streets of the old city, passing mossy-stoned palaces and proud escutcheons, and visited the Mudéjar church of Santa María la Mayor, where in ancient times seafarers lit candles and placed offerings before the statue of Christ. He also browsed among the archeological collections displayed in the former monastery of Santo Domingo. With perfect timing, he then watched the sun set over Combarro, a pretty fishing village with gray-roofed houses and green fishing nets.

The landscape around Combarro, bathed in sunlight.

BAIONA

When the sea mist had dispersed and the clear morning sun shone, the traveler, who had slept in a castle in a spacious room with a canopied bed, leaned out of the window to take in the sea view. Opposite the promontory, as the mist gradually cleared, the three green-topped granite cliffs of the Cíes Islands began to take shape. After breakfast, the traveler took a small dinghy and skimmed over limpid waters to San Martiño, the southernmost of the three islands, which rises in the middle of the bay. It is named after the Benedictine monastery that once stood there. It was also large enough to accommodate a whale factory from the days when the brave Cantabrian harpooners ventured out into the unknown in search of the great cetacean: "There she blows!"

On his way back to the Parador Conde de Gondomar, the traveler walked along the barbican that stands at the end of the isthmus and defends the tiny cliff-edged peninsula. Seen from the high belvedere, the promontory looks like a green balcony overlooking the ocean or a robust vessel cutting

The Parador Conde de Gondomar, in Baiona, Pontevedra. In the Middle Ages, Baiona was one of Galicia's major ports.

BAIONA

The fort of Monte Real houses the Parador Conde de Gondomar. It is named in memory of the Permanent Governor of Monte Real, Don Diego Sarmiento de Acuña, Count of Gondomar and Spanish ambassador at the court of James I of England between 1612 and 1623.

The parador stands on the site of a former Franciscan monastery; all that remains of the monastery is the dome of the Capilla Mayor, which now serves as the sumptuous ceiling over the hall and main staircase of the parador.

In 140 BC, the people of Baiona, led by Viriato, defeated the Roman legions at the foot of the fortress walls. With the invention of the cannon, the walls were reinforced so as to enable them to withstand this new threat. Besides serving as a bulwark, these reinforced walls also provided a gallery along which cannons could be rolled whenever the fortress needed to be defended. On March 1 1493 the caravel *La Pinta* reached the port of Baiona with news of the discovery of the New World.

through the waves and striving to drag the continent along behind it.

The parador is located within the walls of an ancient castle, which provided hospitality for such heroes of old as Viriato, the Lusitanian warrior who held the Romans in check, or al-Mansur, the great Moorish general who conquered Compostela and Barcelona. Picking his way among the black cannons that had defended the citadel in the 18th century, the traveler imagined how awestruck the first Native American must have been as, arriving from America in the caravel *La Pinta*, he contemplated the walls and defenses, the paved roads, and the horses. The ship, returning from Columbus's first voyage, reached land on these beaches in the spring of 1493. The unfortunate man died shortly afterward and was given a Christian burial in Baiona.

In the afternoon, after the restorative siesta that followed a gargantuan lunch – lobster and rice, Moaña-style veal, and *filloas* in a cream sauce – the traveler explored his lodgings. The building is a warren of rooms and corridors, of patios and stairways, in which meld different historical epochs and architectural styles. The walls are set with towers – the Terrace Tower, Clock Tower, and Prince's Tower – which date from the 10th century. The Prince's Tower is named after an Austrian noble who was imprisoned for life within its walls. Neither his

Above and opposite page: *Monte Real,*
the fortress at Baiona that today houses
the Parador Conde de Gondomar.

identity nor the reason for his fate were ever known, for the prisoner never spoke and his face was permanently hidden behind an iron mask. Local elders affirm that the ghost of the mysterious prisoner still prowls through the castle and its grounds, and that on moonlit nights he can be glimpsed in the distance, scanning the horizon as if expecting someone's arrival.

ZAMORA

It was a bright, cheerful sunny morning, and the traveler continued on his way, the only question on his mind being whether to enter Zamora by way of the stone bridge or the iron bridge.

Zamora is a Romanesque rather than a Gothic city. However, the traveler chose to stay in a 15th-century palace that had been converted into a parador. The walls of the original castle have witnessed much bloodshed and much history. It was built in 1459 by the first duke of Aliste, uncle of Ferdinand V of Castile, on the ruins of a Moorish fortress. The castle was destroyed a century later during the war of the *comuneros*, in which the Castilian nobility rose up against Charles V, king of Spain and Holy Roman Emperor. It was later rebuilt as a palace by the fourth duke of Aliste, in an Italian Renaissance style moderated by Castilian sobriety. The traveler was at a loss to know what to admire the most: the magnificent staircase built by the duke or the fine German suits of armor for knights and horses that were displayed on the landing. The room that he had been given, located off one of the elegant galleries framing the Renaissance patio, was hung with tapestries made in the royal workshops. The

room overlooked the square where, during Holy Week in Zamora, a city famous for its piety and religious observance, the *Miserere* is held.

Wandering through the streets of the old part of the city, between austere palaces and ancient town houses, the traveler came eventually to the former sentry walk, between the Duero river and the turreted walls of the old city. Here, beneath the shade of a poplar, he ran into a group of people strolling about the city as he was, and they began chatting together.

"That small gate that you see there is the Postigo de la Traición, where Bellido Dolfos, King Sancho's assassin, found refuge in the city from the hot pursuit of El Cid Campeador."

Opposite page and below: *two views of the Parador Condes de Alba y Alieste, in Zamora, showing elements of the old palace, an important example of Castilian-Leonese architecture.*

ZAMORA

The parador is housed in the palace built in 1459 by the first duke of Alba and Aliste. The palace is considered to be one of the finest surviving examples of Castilian-Leonese civic architecture. During the war of the *comuneros* the building suffered serious damage; it was restored by the fourth duke of Alba and Aliste in the Renaissance style that was fashionable at the time. A notable feature of the building is the main courtyard, its double arcade decorated with medallions featuring mythological and heraldic motifs.

"He was probably not such a traitor as he was supposed to have been," another butted in. "The thing is, Don Sancho had besieged Zamora because he planned to snatch the city away from his sister, the Infanta, who had legally inherited it from her father."

A heated debate began, some arguing in favor of the Infanta and others in favor of Don Sancho. The traveler took his leave of the learned company and continued on his way, climbing up narrow streets until he reached the cathedral. Here he much admired the building's Byzantine dome, Gothic sanctuary, and classical façade.

That night, as he watched the light of the setting sun shimmering on the Duero and its grassy banks, he understood why the Arab name for Zamora – *Samurah* – means "city of turquoise."

The interior of the Parador Condes de Alba y Alieste.

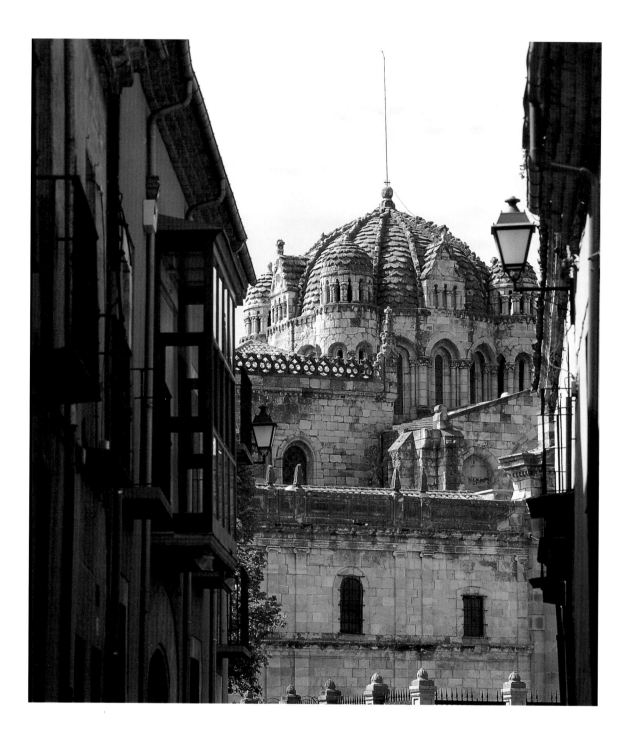

The church of San Juan, Zamora, built in the
Romanesque style of the late 12th
to early 13th centuries.

Zamora Cathedral: a view of the elegant
dome over the transept.

When Spain was a Roman province, Zamora was
known as Ocellum Duri, *"the eye of the Duero."*

CIUDAD RODRIGO

et me tell you that here lived Doña
María Alfonso, otherwise known as
La Coronada. She was such a virtuous
woman that, when she was courted by Juan II of
Castile, and pressed by his illicit amorous advances,
she saw no possible way of rebuffing such an
illustrious gentleman, so she poured boiling oil over
her face and breasts, saying: 'God forbid that on your
account I commit such a vile mortal sin.' Doña María
Coronel is supposed to have done the same in Seville.

*A view of Ciudad Rodrigo, Salamanca.
Many town houses, emblazoned with coats
of arms, are still to be seen in the city.*

*The Parador Enrique II, in Ciudad
Rodrigo. The town was known as
Augustóbriga in Roman times.*

Who knows? Perhaps that was what people did in those days.

As he drank his coffee, the traveler, awestruck by such a terrible story, reflected on the fortitude of individuals – and that of cities. He was relaxing in a leather armchair in the sunlit salon of the Parador Enrique II in Ciudad Rodrigo. This parador is located in the converted citadel of a frontier city that once defended the border against the Moors and the kingdom of Portugal; it is a city with warlike origins but in these more stable times its beauties can be enjoyed as the mellow fruits of peace.

The citadel in Ciudad Rodrigo is a great fortified tower around which cluster residential quarters, which were built in the 14th century by Enrique II de Trastámara. They are plain without

CIUDAD RODRIGO

This parador, within the walls of a castle, has welcomed travelers since 1929. It is set on a cliff overlooking the plain of the Agueda river, and in medieval Latin chronicles it is referred to as *Mirobriga Vettorum*. The area was conquered by Alfonso VI. Only scant vestiges of the original fortress remain. The castle that now stands on the site was built by Henry II, known as Enrique II de Trastámara, illegitimate son of Alfonso XI of Castile, after the bitter civil war in which he killed his stepbrother, the legitimate king Pedro the Cruel.

Traces of Roman building can be discerned in the mighty walls of the castle of Ciudad Rodrigo.

but luxuriously appointed within. The walls of the high corridors are hung with tapestries and armor, and furnished with cabinets and other interesting antique pieces. Its thick crenelated walls, covered with ivy, are reflected in the still waters of the Agueda river.

On the advice of an experienced fellow-diner, the traveler lunched on *farinato*, a substantial local sausage, followed by a dessert of honey and cream cheese.

"How was that?"

"Very tasty."

"Pity you weren't here some years ago, because then you could have tried our local green lizard stew, a dish fit for the gods that we can't make anymore since the beast was declared a protected species."

The traveler idly considered the privations and restrictions imposed by modern life (which, being a disciplined individual, he accepted), then spent the afternoon exploring the city's streets; this was food for the spirit. He especially liked the great starry dome of the cathedral and the tombs of ancient warriors and of noblemen and noblewomen in chapels and niches, with each seeming more beautiful and more richly ornamented than the last.

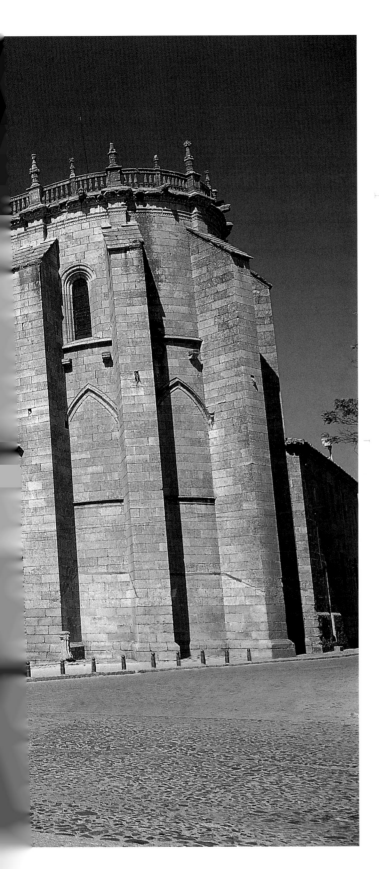

As another day dawned, he visited the Peña de Francia, where Rodrigo, the Visigothic king and the last of his line, retired to live as a hermit. He had raped the daughter of Don Julián, governor of Ceuta, and the outraged father took his revenge by allowing the Moors to disembark in Spain. Thus a moment's lust became the price of a whole kingdom. The unfortunate Rodrigo buried himself alive in a sepulcher, with a fearsome snake; his cries of anguish are echoed in an old Castilian ballad:

Ya me come, ya me come
por do más pecado había...
(It devours me, it devours me
for my terrible sins...)

Considering the terrible consequences that occasionally arise from thoughtless acts, the traveler retired for a peaceful night's sleep.

Ciudad Rodrigo Cathedral, which was founded by
Ferdinand II in the 12th century, when the west front
was begun.

Above: *the city hall.*

Jarandilla de la Vera

« *Lo mejor de España es la Vera; lo mejor de la Vera es Jarandilla ... Allí está lo mejor del mundo. Y allí quisiera que me enterrasen para irme al cielo.* » (The best of Spain is La Vera; the best of La Vera is Jarandilla... The best in the world is there. And I should like to be buried there so that I may go to Heaven.) Thus was Jarandilla de la Vera eulogized by Charles V, Holy Roman Emperor, in his day the most powerful man on earth and the most widely traveled of his time.

Jarandilla de la Vera is like an orchard set amid verdant valleys. The area's abundant springs produce torrents that rush impetuously through gorges, but their fury quickly dies when their waters calm as they reach fertile vegetable gardens and shady groves. This part of Spain, a kind of paradise, has been populated since ancient times; anyone who explores the area will see that it is dotted with Roman roads and bridges, and medieval buildings. The church of Jarandilla, built by the Knights Templar, contains a baptismal font carved with the ancient sign of the swastika.

It was on the ruins of the former fortress built by the Knights Templar that, between the late 14th and early 15th centuries, the dukes of Oropesa and the marquises of Jarandilla, lords of the land, built the castle which today is a parador. In designing the building, the architect followed the canons of the Italian Renaissance, the fashion of the time; somewhat like a prickly pear, the castle has a tough, thorny outer aspect that conceals the sweetness of gracious living within. From without, Jarandilla Castle appears as a quadrangular fortress with a drawbridge, machicolations, embrasures, and robust corner turrets; within these fortifications, however, is an oasis of peace and beauty – a Renaissance palace arranged around a courtyard in which ivy, cypresses,

JARANDILLA DE LA VERA

This fortified palace was begun in the late 14th century by Don García Álvarez de Toledo, Marquis of Jarandilla, duke of Oropesa and maestre of Santiago. Work on the castle, interrupted by long periods of inactivity, continued for almost a century. Typical of fortified palaces built in Europe in the Italian style, the castle has a square ground plan and its central feature is a courtyard lined with a double arcade, with segmented arches below and basket-handle arches above.

Between November 1565 and February 1567 the castle served as the residence of the Holy Roman Emperor Charles V while work was carried out on his final residence and place of retirement, the monastery of San Jerónimo at Yuste, nearby.

and palms harmoniously entwine and where the dancing, crystalline waters of the central fountain contrast with the static beauty of the double Gothic arcade and beautiful stone balcony.

Beneath these robust timber beams and on the brick-paved floors walked the gout-ridden and prematurely aged figure of Charles V, lord of two worlds, who, disillusioned with the pomp and splendor of power, relinquished the imperial crown in 1558 to retire and live a placid old age in the secluded gardens of La Vega. In fact, the Holy Roman Emperor's final residence was to be the monastery of San Jerónimo at nearby Yuste (just over 4 miles away), but while his living quarters were being built there, he settled here in Jarandilla Castle. Charles brought with him his indispensable retinue of cooks, master brewers, confessors, secretaries, and escorts. He had renounced worldly ostentation, but not his legendary gluttony. He even had brought to La Vega live oysters and different varieties of pickled fish. We may assume also that such a demanding

sybarite would have discovered additional delights in the local traditional cuisine: the wild asparagus, garden produce, roast kid, nourishing soups, cheesecakes and, above all, the famous Piornal hams and the excellent Extremaduran *embutidos* (stuffed, spiced pig's bladder). The ubiquitous pig, great star of the regional cuisine, inspired this popular and tasty little rhyme:

> *Seis cosas hubo en la boda de Antón:*
> *cerdo, cochino, puerco, marrano, guarro y lechón*
> ("At Antón's wedding feast there were six different things to eat." Then follow six different words for "pig" in Spanish.)

On still autumn afternoons, while the rain fell outside, the Emperor who had fought against the Lutherans and the Pope, who had crossed the ocean five times, would recall his travels and battles, his conquests of cities and lovers, huddled before the hearth in his oak armchair, which can still be seen in the parador. During the long winter nights, a local minstrel would entertain him by singing ballads of La Serrana de la Vera, the legendary mountain woman who murdered travelers after raping them and whose hideaway, in the neighboring Garganta de la Olla, can still be visited today. Nearby is the house known as the Casa de las Muñecas (Dolls' House), the discreet house of pleasure, where the emperor's entourage would while away their leisure hours in the company of prostitutes. It is not hard to understand why one of these courtiers defined La Vera as "the best place for repose and for the pleasures of mind and body."

Previous pages and right: *the castle at Jarandilla de la Vera, Cáceres, was the temporary residence of Charles V after his abdication and before he settled in the monastery of San Jerónimo del Yuste, nearby. It has now been restored and converted into the Parador Charles V.*

Following pages: *The swimming pool within the walls of the castle, now the Parador Charles V. Interior views of the Parador Charles V.*

OROPESA

Oropesa, like the nymphs that haunted the fountains in ancient times, sings an ancient song and draws wayfarers to itself as they pass on the highroad. The traveler, following the course of Tagus, like so many other travelers in times gone by, had spent the morning visiting the collegiate church of Talavera de la Reina – a Mudéjar building described by some as Byzantine-Romanesque – and examining the local blue ceramics. He had wanted to continue investigating the local ceramics, and had planned to look at the green pottery of Puente del Arzobispo; but back on the road through Extremadura he caught sight of Oropesa castle, an enticing silhouette that rose up in the distance, atop a gently rolling hill, and he could not resist the temptation of ending his day's journey there. He had also read Somerset Maugham, and perhaps the thought of Oropesa had conjured up these words:

"I had intended only to lunch there, but I found the place so inviting that I decided to stay for some time."

People often find a compelling interest in following in the footsteps of the authors whom they have read, to see what they saw and tread the roads they trod: this is another way, no less subtle than reading itself, of living out the experiences of literature. Perhaps Somerset Maugham himself had paused in Oropesa while following in the tracks of two great authors: St Teresa of Ávila and St John of the Cross.

Oropesa consists of two castles, the Old and the New. The buildings are separated by a wall crowned by a machicolated parapet. The New Castle is now a parador. The Old Castle guarded the road from Extremadura to the Meseta during the Reconquista and also during the 14th century, when Pedro the Cruel, king of Castile and León, and his illegitimate brother Enrique de Trastámara fought for possession

OROPESA

The actual castle occupies the eastern half of a trapezium-shaped site, while the palace occupies the other half. The keep is a typical 15th-century fortification, and the parts of the castle built from regular ashlars date from the same period. These stand in marked contrast to the masonry of the older ruins on which the present-day fortress was built. A magnificent machicolated parapet runs along the dividing wall. The keep's sentry boxes bear two sets of coats of arms, one those of Fernando Álvarez de Toledo, fourth lord of Oropesa, who died in 1462, and the other those of his wife, Leonor de Zúñiga.

Opposite page: *the Parador of Oropesa
by night.*

Above: *the walls of Oropesa castle. From this fortress,
the* comuneros *fought against the troops of the Holy
Roman Emperor Charles V.*

Previous pages: *two views of the courtyard of the
Parador de Oropesa.*

of the throne. The vestiges of the Old Castle are
chiefly confined to the eastern tower. In the
15th century, stones from the Old Castle were reused
to build the New Castle, in the Mudéjar style.
A century later, the building was extended with
palatial additions in the peculiarly intricate Spanish
Renaissance style known as Plateresque. The castle's
new lord, Don Francisco Álvarez de Toledo, duke of
Alba, duke of Oropesa, fifth viceroy of Peru, and
founder of the city of Cochabamba, converted one of
the wings of the New Castle into a palace equipped
with all the comforts of the time: the façade, pierced
by more than 100 balconies, windows, arrow slits,
and embrasures, was austere; within, there were
spacious halls, glazed brick floors, grand staircases,
courtyards, dependencies, corridors, rooms, and
coffered ceilings. The traveler admired the octagonal
room built of dressed ashlars and known as the
Peinador de la Reina (Queen's Boudoir), the Mudéjar
coffering that graces the castle's dining room and

halls, and the Baroque sculptures that faithfully reflect the twisted spirituality of the age of the Council of Trent and the Inquisition.

Having taken a well-lit room with a vaulted ceiling, from which he could admire a landscape of hills, wheat fields and woodland, with the Sierra de Gredos in the distance, the traveler ate a lunch of rabbit pie seasoned with thyme and washed down with a full-bodied Rueda wine.

The traveler then made his way to the old castle. Climbing the keep he discovered a deadly trap that the architect had set: anyone who forced entry at the bottom could not reach the floor above by means of the staircase without exposing himself to a shower of enemy arrows from the sentry walk outside, and even if he managed to reach the walk he would have to cross a wooden floor, removable in case of danger, leading to the stairs. In the evening the traveler set off for Lagarteras, a tiny village where the embroiderers are among the best in the world.

W. Somerset Maugham is thought to have spent some time in Oropesa, following in the footsteps of writers from times gone by. On this voyage of discovery, the author felt himself to be treading the very same soil as, in very different times, had trod St Teresa or San Juan de la Cruz.

The Parador Virrey de Toledo, seen from the surrounding olive groves.

CÁCERES

The words "This is the house of the Golfines" are chiseled into the wall of the parador, within a cartouche. Above is the family coat of arms, set within an elaborate crest from which emerges a hand holding a dagger. The traveler, suddenly transported back to the 14th century, entered the parador.

The Parador de Cáceres is something of a labyrinth. It consists of several contiguous buildings:

Opposite page: the Parador of Cáceres combines medieval and Renaissance styles of architecture.

Below: the Parador de Cáceres by night.

the palace of the Marquis and Marchioness of Torreorgaz, and the ancestral homes of several lesser nobles – the Ovandos, Mogollones, Pereos, and Paredes. Some of the walls are bare stone, polished with the patina of time; others are more recently whitewashed. It is hard to tell where one building ends and another begins, or which parts are medieval and which Renaissance additions. But the traveler felt very much at home in this patchwork of rooms and panoply of architectural styles; penetrating into the depths of the parador, he set off to explore its maze of passages, corridors, staircases, and courtyards. Here he looked out of a Gothic window, there he glimpsed a secluded patio through lead-framed stained glass. On the landing of one of the staircases he marveled at the precise beauty of a painted wooden carving.

CÁCERES

The parador is housed within the fortified palace of the Torreorgaz family, built around 1488 by Don Diego García de Ulloa, *comendador* of Alcuescar and one of the Knights of St James. It stands on the site of older Moorish buildings, of which few vestiges remain. The successive building phases can be read in the walls. The medieval part is rubblework and the Renaissance section is built of ashlars.

The former palace of the Marquis and Marchioness of Torreorgaz is today a welcoming and comfortable parador.

The old city of Cáceres, within the ancient Almohad walls, invites exploration.

Finally he returned to the lounge, where relaxing in a soft leather armchair he admired the coffered ceiling, decorated with restful plant motifs.

The traveler now took in the convent-like peace of this great monumental city, which had always stood on a perilous frontier. As he wandered the narrow medieval streets that wind around the city's center, he admired the endless succession of ancestral homes and monasteries, of churches and towers that make Cacéres one of Europe's great architectural cities.

Cáceres is encircled by an Almohad wall, built

of stones that one day would be trodden by the two great Conquistadors who came from this region: Francisco de Orellana, who was lost in the jungles of America while searching for El Dorado, the mythical city where the roofs of houses were tiled with gold; and Francisco Pizarro, who together with a handful of adventurers conquered Peru and founded Lima.

Somewhat weary after his walk, the traveler lunched on a restorative gazpacho, here known as *cojondongo*, followed by homemade sweets prepared by the hands of the pure young nuns of the convent of San Pablo.

TRUJILLO

The traveler approached the city forewarned by some lines that he had jotted down in his notebook:

Si fueras a Trujillo, por donde entrares
hallarás una legua de berrocales
(However you approach Trujillo
you will come across a league of granite crags)

His route had taken him over dark granite crags – the very same over which Roman legions and Saracen raiding parties had marched and scrambled;

today they are the domain of the humble kermes oak, the cork oak, and the lordly holm oak, the ground beneath the trees sprinkled with acorns and rich with truffles – delicacies for the Iberian boar. Entering Trujillo, a city of many towers, the traveler found himself in the middle of one of the most beautiful squares in the world, where he paid his respects to a great bronze statue of Pizarro. Mrs Carlos Rumsey, the American who had funded the statue, insisted that the conquistador be depicted as tall and debonair. Having no choice but to comply with her wishes, the sculptor was unable to remain faithful to the truth by depicting Pizarro as he really was: squat and ugly.

TRUJILLO

The building was constructed in 1533 as a convent for nuns of the order of the Immaculate Conception. Like a great many enclosed convents, this one was built in the style of a traditional Moorish palace, which, with its central courtyard, is itself derived from the Roman house. Although the building has an unremarkable exterior, the interior is strikingly beautiful. The courtyard is lined with a Renaissance gallery of rounded arches on pillars beneath a gallery of flat arches supported on Tuscan columns, and a stone parapet pierced with oculi. Trujillo was the birthplace of Conquistadors: among them was Francisco Pizarro, who conquered Peru; Francisco de Orellana, who navigated the Amazon; Francisco de las Casas, who accompanied Cortés on his conquest of Mexico; and Hernando de Alarcón, who explored California.

Opposite page and above: *the Parador de Trujillo, formerly the convent of Santa Clara.*
The simplicity of the building's exterior betrays nothing of the unexpected beauty of the interior.

Trujillo stands on a granite peak (which the Romans called the Fox's Head) and is itself a city built of granite. The ramparts and castle that defended the city, the stones that pave it, and the ashlars that make up the walls and lintels of its ancestral homes, churches, and convents, are all granite.

The traveler, somewhat weary after his journey, approached a local traffic policeman to ask the way to the parador. After a courteous greeting, the officer replied:

"The parador you're asking about is known locally as the convent of Santa Clara, because that is what it originally was. You can't miss it: go down this street, cross the Plazuela de San Miguel, keeping the

Above: *four views of the interior of the Parador de Trujillo. The parador's central courtyard is a comfortable place to take coffee, read newspapers, and think back to the time when novices would read their breviary here.*

Right: *a horseshoe arch in the Parador de Trujillo.*

church on your right, and you'll soon be there."

The traveler recognized the typically southern Spanish architecture, where beauty lies within rather than without. The lobby of the parador still contained the revolving window through which the incarcerated nuns made precarious contact with the outside world, without seeing or being seen.

"Were they so ugly?"

"No, sir, quite the contrary, it seems. Take the founder, for instance, Santa Beatriz de Silva Meneses. She was a friend of Isabella the Catholic and the most beautiful woman of her time."

On his way back to the parador the traveler imagined romantic encounters beneath the granite vaults, in the corridors, and on the stairs of the building. Then, in the cloister surrounded by flat-arched galleries and in the shade of one of the three fountains, he took a refreshing drink.

At lunchtime our friend chose a table at the far end of the dining-room, in an alcove completely covered with trompe l'œil tilework. He had been recommended oxtail and veal stew, "a dish fit for a king." This seemed excellent justification, and the traveler, who loved to try new dishes and was of the opinion that the best that any region can offer is its local stew, did not resist the temptation to try this tasty, regal country fare.

Above: *equestrian statue in Trujillo.*
Opposite page: *the city of Trujillo, set on a granite peak.*

GUADALUPE

There are two places in Spain that may be described as oases. Both have a monastic setting: one is in the monastery of Piedra, in Aragon, and the other in the monastery of Guadalupe, in Extremadura. Guadalupe is surrounded by three mountain ranges – Guadalupe, Altamira, and Villuercas – from which flow streams and rivers that bring abundant, crystal-clear water to the pleasant valleys below; there, thanks to a gentle microclimate, evergreen oaks and chestnuts, oaks and arbutus, olive trees and vines, gall oaks, and rock roses flourish.

"The Virgin didn't choose a bad place to appear before the shepherd."

"No, she certainly didn't."

The Virgin of Guadalupe is a Black Madonna, one of the Black Madonnas that appeared all over Europe throughout the 13th century, a time when the

The patio of the Parador de Guadalupe is filled with the scent of lemon trees and the murmur of running water.

Western world was beginning to reawaken and find a new awareness after the long period of dormancy that followed the fall of the Roman Empire.

The parador where the traveler was staying could not have been more centrally located: right opposite the monastery. This great Mudéjar building, partly religious and partly fortress, belonged originally to the order of St Jerome but is now in the care of the Franciscans. It features a remarkable cloister lined with horseshoe arches and with a Mudéjar shrine in the center. With enthusiasm and much appreciation the traveler visited the church, which is also a royal pantheon, as well as the monastery's library and the museums. Finally, he climbed the Plateresque staircase to admire paintings by Zurbarán, Jordaens, and Carreño.

Guadalupe has been called the baptismal font of the Americas and the monastery of Spanish culture: it has strong links with the Catholic Kings and it was here that, before setting off on his voyages, Columbus commended his soul to the Virgin of Guadalupe. In the monastery of Guadalupe, Ferdinand and Isabella signed letters ordering that Columbus be provided with caravels and the necessary crews, and it was in the font within the monastic cloister that the first two Native Americans to arrive from the other side of the Atlantic were baptised, as Pedro and Juan. The unfortunate men did not live very long, vulnerable as they were to European diseases.

The parador occupies a building that comprises the former Hospital de San Juan Bautista and the adjoining Escuela de Medicina or Colegio de Infantes, a place of "elevated teaching in the virtues and letters." The traveler was shown to a room overlooking the large courtyard, where lemon and orange trees grew in neat rows.

The parador consists of a combination
of two buildings. One was the Hospital
de San Juan Bautista, also known as the
Hospital de Hombres; it was built in the
mid-14th century by the prior Don Toribio
Fernández de Mena, rebuilt in 1402 by
Fray Fernando Yáñez de Figueroa, and
refurbished in the 16th century. The
other was the Colegio de Infantes, built
between 1509 and 1512 by the prior Fray
Juan de Azpeitia for the education of
adolescent boys.

The parador stands opposite the great
monastery of Guadalupe. Its church,
founded in the early 14th century, was
rebuilt in 1336 and enlarged between
1341 and 1367 by order of Alfonso XI, a
devotee of the Black Madonna who is
worshipped here. According to legend, the
Madonna, a small statue carved in oak,
was miraculously found by the shepherd Gil
Cordero beside the Guadalupe river over
600 years after it had been hidden there by
a group of Christians from Seville who were
fleeing northward to escape persecution by
the Moors.

Above: *the interior of the parador of Guadalupe.*

Right: *ogee arches line the courtyard of the parador.*

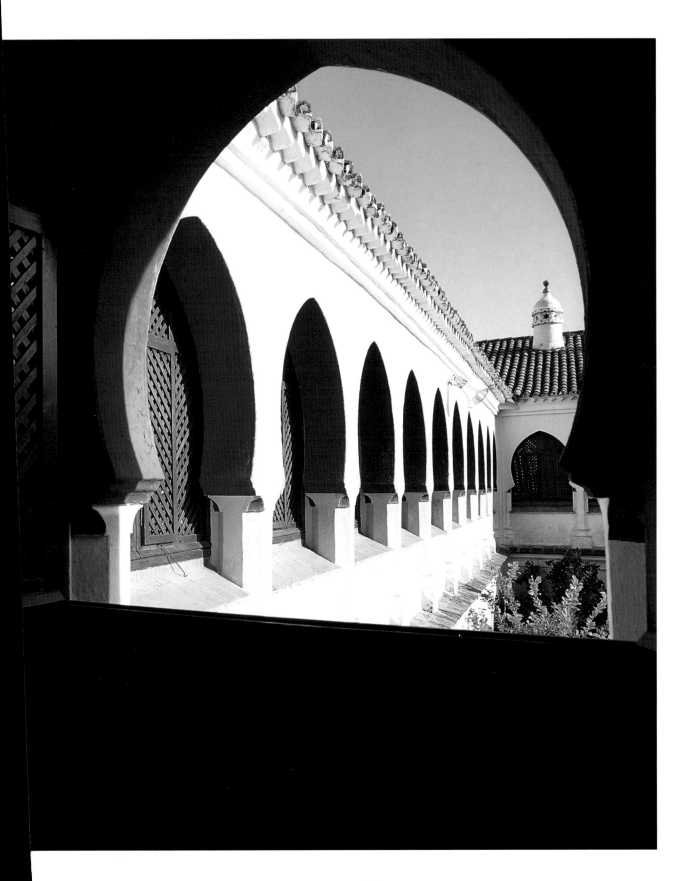

The monastery of Guadalupe, a major center of culture and learning up until the 17th century.
Its main façade presents a magnificent display of 15th-century Gothic tracery.

MÉRIDA

In the whitewashed patio of the parador in Mérida, seated in an ornate cast-iron chair in the pale morning sun, the traveler looked up from the book that he was reading; his gaze alighted on the white belfry before him. No bells hung there but, through the belfry's empty arches, two identical patches of clear blue sky could be seen. A pair of storks had built a large nest on the belfry, right next to the cross that pointed up into the sky. For a while the traveler was engrossed in the observation of their daily lives, watching the mother come and go with her beak full of grubs to feed her hatchlings. Meanwhile, in pages of the book that lay open on the traveler's knees, a 13th-century Arab author was describing Mérida as "the city that captivates us as it captivated the Romans." The succession of cultures that define Mérida could be read even in the courtyard in which the traveler was sitting; Christian master-builders had used Roman and Visigothic stones to build the Mudéjar columns of the courtyard.

The traveler felt captive in Mérida, the famous Emerita Augusta so highly prized by Roman emperors. That morning he had walked across the 60-arch Roman viaduct over the Guadiana, built of granite in the 1st century and later guarded by a Moorish fortress; he had attended a rehearsal of *Medea* in the Roman arena; and, strolling through the melancholy ruins of the nearby amphitheater, in the clamorous silence of the crumbling tiers of stone seats, he had reflected on the fleeting nature of life. In a restaurant on the Plaza Mayor, he had lunched on *caldereta*, the typical lamb stew of Extremadura, followed by cream cheese drizzled with honey; this he ate as a homage to Virgil, the greatest of all Roman poets, who in his *Georgics* wrote "*et durae quercus saludabunt roscida mella*" ("and honeydew oozed from the hard evergreen oaks").

The parador that the visitor had chosen for this stay in Mérida was an 18th-century Franciscan monastery; the basement, under the foundations of the church, contained the refectory, various rooms, and the cells, and beneath the blossoming trellises of the courtyards, the vestiges of the Roman forum and the Temple of Concord, later to be replaced first by a mosque and then by a Christian church. After the friars abandoned it, the building became successively a hospital, a mental asylum, and a jail.

Below and opposite page: *exterior and interior views of the Parador Vía de la Plata, in Mérida.*

MÉRIDA

The parador in Mérida occupies the former monastery of San Francisco, a fine Baroque building by Juan de Herrera. The building's fabric incorporates Roman and Visigothic stones and capitals, which document the long history of this important site. Here, on the Vía de la Plata, also stood a Roman praetorium and Temple of Concord. This Roman road, which runs from Mérida to Astorga, is one of the oldest roads in Europe. The name "Plata" is derived from *balatha*, the type of stones with which the road was paved.

Aqueducts like this one, still graceful though now in ruins, show how water was brought to the city. One of the best known is the Acueducto de los Milagros, built in about the 3rd century AD.

Mérida is a city of many splendors. Among the ancient remains of Emerita Augusta, the famous city so highly esteemed by Roman emperors, is the Roman theater, which still retains an impressive air of grandeur.

Previous pages:
The courtyard of the Parador Vía de la Plata, in Mérida.

ZAFRA

It was a bright sunlit day, and as he journeyed down the main highway, with oak-covered hills to left and right, the traveler passed through a landscape in which outcrops of granite rose up, the occasional pine tree grew, and green meadows stretched away, crossed by a small stream. As he walked, these words echoed in the traveler's mind: "Zafra, ancient land, well-endowed with arms and fertile soils."

The traveler was headed south along the Vía de la Plata, perhaps the oldest road in Europe. In ancient times this was the route along which tin from Galicia and Britain was transported on its way to Huelva, the port from which Phoenician sailors shipped it to the avid markets of Mesopotamia and Egypt.

Zafra saw both the splendor of the Roman Empire and the long night of the Middle Ages. It then became the object of contention between Moors and Christians. It regained its former glory in the 15th century, under the dominion of the Figueroas. Lorenzo Suárez de Figueroa, lord of the city, walled it and built the mighty citadel, now the parador in which the traveler was staying.

Don Ciriaco Restrepo, a retired veterinary surgeon and local scholar, who from 9am until 1pm can be found sunning himself in the square, under doctor's orders, told the traveler a couple of things about the parador where he was planning to stay.

"The parador is a castle outside and a palace inside, as you'll see. It's a rectangular castle with a sturdy keep in the middle. Turrets 80 feet high stand at each of the four corners. Then there are two more turrets – more elegant ones – each side of the main gate."

They entered the lobby, where they saw the coats of arms of the Figueroas, dukes of Feria and grandees of Spain.

Don Ciriaco showed the traveler the courtyard and its surrounding arcade:

"Isn't it lovely? A double arcade of three arches, in the purest Renaissance style. The proportions of this architectural scheme, the simple creation of beauty through mathematical formulae, bear the stamp of Juan de Herrera. He built El Escorial for Philip II, who as you know was a cabbalist and a

Above: the Parador Hernán Cortés in Zafra. It was originally a fortified palace, built in 1437.

Right: the parador's Renaissance courtyard, built by Juan de Herrera.

Opposite page and above: *the Parador Hernán Cortés, in Zafra.*

ZAFRA

This fortified palace was built in 1437 by Don Lorenzo Suárez de Figueroa ("the Magnificent"), duke of Feria and Zafra, and a grandee of Spain. In the construction of the palace he used the remains of a Moorish fortress, which had been wrested from the Moors by Ferdinand III. The palace courtyard, with its strictly symmetrical arcade, is a typical example of the work of Juan de Herrera. The building was embellished with marble and jasper brought from Portugal by the first mistress of the palace, Doña María Manuela. The most notable feature of the palace is its Gothic chapel, surmounted by an octagonal dome.

magician. And another thing: it's difficult to imagine that such austerity on the outside of the building could lead to such beauty within."

Don Ciriaco then led the visitor through the former palace of the Figueroas, showing him its many wonders: the dazzling coffered ceiling of the Alcoba Dorada; the vaults of the keep – from its flat roof they took in a panorama of the rooftops of Zafra and the countryside round about; the floors of Portuguese marble brought by Doña María Manuela, duchess of Figueroa; the staircase down which Hernán Cortés walked before setting off to conquer Mexico; the Mudéjar coffered ceiling of the former chapel; the medieval furniture and other objects displayed in the elegant rooms.

Zafra is surrounded by beautiful sights; these the traveler took at a leisurely pace, one by one. In Feria, which he reached after a few miles through a pleasant landscape of woodlands and holm oaks, he visited the castle, and climbed the keep to test the veracity of a local saying: that on a clear day you can see twenty-two villages. Indeed, it was true, and to

celebrate his discovery the traveler repaired to a tavern in the square, where he feasted on scrambled eggs with wild asparagus and a superb *caldereta* (lamb stew). To work off his lunch, he took a stroll around the village; he saw that the local inhabitants had had the good sense to preserve the character of the local vernacular architecture. Later that afternoon he continued his exploration with a visit to the neighboring village of Salvatierra de los Barros; true to its name (*barro* means clay), the village keeps alive a long tradition of pottery-making. As he watched the hands of an expert potter mold soft clay into a vessel on the wheel, the traveler wondered what it is about clay, fire, and the sea that makes them so fascinating and mysterious.

The traveler had had a full day. The next day he went to Jerez de los Caballeros, stopping along the way to see some dolmens. In Jerez, on the advice of Don Ciriaco, he visited the castle. The main tower is known as the "bloody tower" for it was here that the Knights Templar who had defended the castle were beheaded. In the afternoon he strolled through the stone-paved streets of Frenegal de la Sierra, another redoubt of the Knights Templar; here were mansions emblazoned with coats of arms, and the mysterious name "Bafome" carved on the town's main gateway.

Above: *a Neoclassical façade in Zafra.*
Opposite page: *the town of Zafra, and its 15th-century fortress.*

CARMONA

«This was the beloved residence of Pedro the Cruel, and here he took his pleasures. Through its gates came and went the brilliant cavalcades that escorted María de Padilla...». The traveler closed the book, placed it on the table beside his empty cup, and closed his eyes. From the Mudéjar courtyard, enclosed by slender marble columns, came the murmur of water trickling in the central fountain. Golden midday light was filtering through the canopy, creating an unreal atmosphere; the traveler lounged comfortably in his deck chair and let his imagination take flight – back to the time when Pedro I (Pedro the Cruel to some and Pedro the Just to others) built this fortress in Carmona. He saw before him a corpulent man, rather heavy-shouldered but attractive, with the fevered gaze that lovers and lunatics tend to have. He was the son of Alfonso IX of Castile and his childhood was marked by the hatred that his mother, the queen, felt for his father's concubine and for the concubine's sons, Pedro's stepbrothers Enrique, Fadrique, and Tello. When Don Pedro inherited the throne, he furiously persecuted the late king's lover and her illegitimate offspring. However, by one of those twists of fate that result in curious symmetries, he also suffered from the same excesses of the heart as had his father.

For reasons of state, Don Pedro had been married off to a French princess, Blanche de Bourbon, whom he did not love. After their wedding night he fled from her to join his lover, María de Padilla, a slender, sweet-natured, dark-haired woman who had borne him a daughter three months earlier.

The unfortunate Don Pedro spent half his life battling against the rebellious nobility that supported the pretender to the throne, his bastard brother Enrique de Trastámara. He felt quite alone. "A single

CARMONA

The parador is located in the Alcázar de la Puerta de Marchena, one of Carmona's three fortresses, set on the highest point of the hill. The oldest parts of the building, on the far side of the parador's esplanade, date from the Almoravid and Almohad periods (12th and 13th centuries). Pedro the Cruel may have remodeled the fortress considerably in the 14th century. In the 15th century, the fortress were strengthened in the north-west corner by a prominent casemate, known as El Cubete, with two rows of embrasures and a domed roof. This castle played a major role in the conflicts between the duke of Medina Sidonia and the marquis of Cádiz, especially in the siege of 1472.

Opposite page: *entrance to the Parador Alcázar del Rey Don Pedro, in Carmona.*

Above: *the lounge within the parador.*

loaf of bread," he said, "would be enough to fill the bellies of all those who are loyal to me."

Before setting off on his last campaign, with the foreboding of death in his heart, he left his children and his treasures in the castle of Carmona.

As he contemplated what he had been reading, the traveler imagined the king crossing the covered courtyard. He was in full armor, over which he wore a tabard quartered with the somewhat faded arms of Castile: golden towers on a red ground. He was followed by a page bearing the royal helmet crowned by a serpent. Shortly afterward, in Montiel, on a night filled with the light of bonfires and the sound of drums, Pedro, who was besieged behind the

crumbling fortress battlements, kept a secret appointment with his stepbrother and adversary to discuss a peace treaty. Pages led him to the tent of Enrique, the illegitimate pretender. The two brothers exchanged a cold but courteous greeting; then they got down to business, only to discover that irreconcilable differences lay between what the besieger was demanding and what the besieged was prepared to concede.

A heated argument ensued, which then led to a fight, the two men rolling on the ground with daggers drawn. In the flickering light, when Pedro was on the point of overpowering his brother, the French mercenary Beltrán Duguesclin took hold of the king so that Enrique could run him through. "I neither make nor unmake kings," he said, "I simply serve my lord."

The castle and parador of Carmona stand on a hill overlooking plains that flank the Carbones river. The landscape stretches for miles to the hazy blue horizon. There is no richer land than this south of the Pyrenees. For this Carmona has been highly prized by a succession of inhabitants: Tartesians, Turdetanians, Phoenicians, Carthaginians, Romans, Moors, and Christians. As the old saying goes, "*Villa por Villa, Carmona en Andalucía*" (There's no better town than Carmona in Andalusia), or according to another, "*Carmona, quienes la tuvieron, ricos fueron; quienes la tienen, bien se mantienen*" (Those who held Carmona were rich; those who hold her now live well).

The traveler had lunched on scrambled eggs with locally grown asparagus and wild rabbit with mushrooms. As he took his siesta, the traveler had been lulled by the murmur of the fountain in the Mudéjar courtyard. Later he had strolled through the city's gently meandering streets and alleyways and, in the quiet of the afternoon, had admired its Baroque palaces, especially those of Aguilar and Rueda, with their tall, lace-curtained windows and wide, well-kept walks. There was also the impressive urban complex of the Plaza de San Fernando, surrounded by fine 16th-century buildings, one or two Baroque palaces, and a few 19th-century mansions. The square presents a stimulating combination of decorative tilework, marble columns, and arcaded

Opposite page and above: *three different views of the Parador Alcázar del Rey Don Pedro, in Carmona.*

galleries; particularly noteworthy is the Mudéjar house on its western side, which is decorated with Cuenca tiles. The traveler had also visited the convent of Santa Clara, with its paintings by Valdés Leal, the Baroque church of El Salvador, with its impressive high altar, and the church of San Pedro, with Gothic baptismal fonts faced with glazed tiles. In the courtyard of Santa María, which was once attached to a mosque, the traveler came across a Visigothic almanac carved on a column shaft.

Exploring the interesting Carthaginian necropolis, comprising 800 tombs, he had sought the enigmatic Tomb of the Elephant, which included three dining rooms and a kitchen, and the Tomb of the Rich Servilia, as spacious as a patrician's town house. He had visited the three citadels, an upper one – known as Puerta de Sevilla, the finest Carthaginian stronghold in the West and even in the East – and two lower ones.

When, while still a prince, Don Pedro had fallen in love with Carmona, he found in the town nothing more than a gloomy Roman and Visigothic castle; it was an agglomeration of crumbling rooms, stables, stores, barracks, and workshops. On the site of this ugly pile of fortifications he built courtyards, rebuilt walls, and created belvederes which let in air and light and towered over the surrounding wheat fields, olive groves, orchards, woods, and paved walkways. To decorate the interior of his residence, he sent for Moorish master builders from Granada, the same ones who had sculpted the magnificent façade of the *alcázar* of Seville. He installed glazed tiles, marble fountains, and inlaid ceilings. Neglect and decay have taken their toll on the condition of the palace, and earthquakes have sent some of the towers toppling over into the precipice below. Nevertheless, the traveler noticed that after recent restoration the building was returning to its original state of grace and nobility, and becoming once again the idyllic palace so beloved by Don Pedro.

Thanks to a program of rebuilding, the former palace of Pedro the Cruel, in Carmona, has been restored to the elegant Mudéjar dwelling that it was in the days of Pedro.

GRANADA

From the balcony of his room, the traveler looked out over the Generalife, the summer palace of the kings of Granada. Had he taken lodgings on the opposite side, he would have enjoyed views of the Albaicín, the Moorish quarter, with its red roofs, white walls, and secretive courtyards marked out by the lance-like tops of cypress trees. In the distance, the perpetual snows of the Sierra Nevada sparkled in the sunlight, while Mount Mulhacén stood out clearly against the limpid blue sky.

This parador, the traveler thought, must be the most blessed place on earth. It was the Franciscan monastery of the Alhambra, built in the 15th century by Isabella the Catholic to fulfill a promise.

Queen Isabella had never promised not to change her blouse until Granada had been conquered, as some suggest. What she had promised

The parador was built on the site of a Franciscan monastery founded by the Catholic Kings. Just as Isabella of Castile had promised, the monastery's church was built next to the Moorish palaces.

Views of the courtyard and interior of the parador in Granada.

was to build this monastery and its church beside the Moorish palaces. Once again the traveler felt mesmerized by the sheer variety and combination of decorative elements: the ceilings and the tilework, the geometrical order of the patio and the belvederes, all bore the stamp of the skilled craftsmanship of Moslem master builders. The paintings, sculptures, and tapestries that hung from the walls formed part of the alterations carried out by the Christians when they built their church on the ruins of the Moorish aristocracy's civic buildings.

The monastery of San Francisco stands on the site of a mosque and Moorish palace with garden and baths that Yussuf I built between 1332 and 1364. Until a permanent mausoleum had been built in the city's cathedral, the monastery church temporarily housed the tomb of Ferdinand and Isabella.

Granada, where the magic of the East is transported to a Western setting, is a supremely romantic city. If all Moslems must make the pilgrimage to Mecca at least once in their lives, all travelers must make at least one visit to the Alhambra.

The Alhambra (from the Arabic *al hamra* – the Red One – after the color of its walls) comprises a castle and five palaces – four Moorish and one Christian. The Moorish palaces were built between the 13th and 15th centuries by the last Moorish dynasty in Spain. The Christian palace is a sturdy building in the Italian Renaissance style that Charles V, grandson of the Catholic Kings, grafted onto the open side of the Alhambra.

The traveler spent all morning wandering through the maze of rooms, patios, gardens, and chambers. He was particularly taken by the Ambassadors' Room, also known as the Throne Room, where the cedarwood dome illustrates the

The parador in Granada. Doors open onto rooms that seem to be filled with mystery.

firmament. The monarchs of Granada had their throne installed in one of the niches cut into the massively thick walls, with their backs turned toward the balcony. This was so that the light coming from behind plunged their faces into semidarkness, and the ambassador or courtier summoned before the sovereigns could not discern the expression on the royal faces.

From the height of the belvedere, the traveler looked out over Granada, the city which in the dying days of Moorish Spain, the sultanate split into factions; at their peril the Moors overlooked the Christian troops assembled at their gates.

The visitor next found himself in the Court of Lions, whose geometrically ordered design represents an earthly paradise. In the Sala de los Abencerrajes, the traveler looked upon a faded bloodstain (it might have been oxidization in the

GRANADA

The parador is located within a Franciscan monastery founded by the Catholic Kings when they conquered Granada in 1492. The site was formerly occupied by a mosque and a palace built by the 14th-century sultan Yussuf I. The gardens and belvederes of the parador command a view of the towers of the Alhambra, the fountains of the Generalife, the red walls of the Albaicín, and the snow-covered peaks of the Sierra Nevada.

Above: *a view of the Alhambra and, below, the Court of Lions.*
Opposite page: *Kufic script sings the praises of Allah.*

marble) that, according to tradition, marks the spot
where the Abencerrajes, one of the dynasties that
fought for power in Granada, were murdered. While
the Christians were throwing bridges over the
irrigation ditches in the fields to bring in their heavy
artillery, the courtesans of Granada were plotting in
favor of Boabdil, or of his father the dethroned king,
or of his uncle.

The traveler fancied that he saw the Alhambra
through the eyes of Boabdil, the last king of Granada,
who surrendered his city to the Christians. He had
been deeply moved by the tale of the king's
farewell and subsequent banishment. As Boabdil
contemplated the towers, palaces, and groves of the
city, he could contain himself no longer and burst
into tears. Then his mother, Queen Aixa, spoke to
him in harsh and terrible terms: "Weep, weep like a
woman for what you have failed to defend as a man!"

JAÉN

Jaén castle stretches out like an old lizard in the sun on the rocky crest of the hill of Santa Catalina. These imposing heights tower over a wide landscape: on one side is the stony mass of Jabalcuz; on the other, waves of rolling hills covered with olive groves that, in the pure air and beneath the vault of a clear blue sky, stretch away to the distant Sierra Mágina, on the far side of the Guadalquivir valley. Because of its frontier position, this land of white villages and green mountains has been called *Guarda y Defendimiento de los Reinos de Castilla* (Guardian and Defender of the Kingdoms of Castile). As he made his way through the olive groves, the traveler's thoughts turned to the great battles – of Baécula, Navas de Tolosa, and Bailén, the most decisive in the history of the Iberian peninsula – that had been fought here within an area of just a few square miles.

Opposite page and above: *the Parador Castillo de Santa Catalina, Jaén. It was built by Fernando III,*
as part of his campaign against the Moors. Today, access to the citadel is less steep.

Few European castles can boast of such a heroic past as that of Jaén. The original castle, a caliphs' fortress, was built in the 9th century and later played a crucial role in the civil wars between the different *taifas* (petty kingdoms) that formed after the collapse of the caliphate. Around 1130, Jaén castle was enlarged by the Almoravids, a powerful tribe from the Sahara who conquered North Africa and occupied Moorish Spain. The castle, now a huge rectangular fortress defended by many identical, closely set towers, was remodeled in the mid-13th century by Alfonso X, the Wise, after his father Ferdinand III, the Saint, had won back the city.

Alfonso X divided the castle into two precincts; this provided him with a second, more easily defended refuge in case of emergency. In this latter precinct, he extended the walls so as to close off the area known as the Alcázar Nuevo; it was then separate from the rest of the Almoravid fortress

JAÉN

The Parador Castillo de Santa Catalina stands on the site of a Moorish fortress. The present castle was built in the mid-13th century by Alfonso X, the Wise, on a caliph's alcazaba (citadel), which had been previously extended by the Almoravids. The keep of the Christian fort is one of the finest in Andalusia. The castle suffered damage both in the frontier wars between Christians and Moors and the Castilian civil wars during the reign of Henry IV. During the War of Independence it was a Napoleonic troops prison.

The Parador del Castillo de Santa Catalina invites rest and reflection on the great battles of the Reconquista,
such as those of Bailén and Navas de Tolosa.

(known from then on as the Alcázar Viejo). Between the two precincts, he built a sturdy wall and an imposing keep.

When the Catholic Kings conquered Granada in 1492, the twin fortresses of Jaén lost their military importance. However, a garrison remained stationed there until well into the 18th century. In the 19th century Jaén castle was occupied by Napoleonic troops, and it was temporarily restored to its former glory: they built a prison and a garrison in the castle, and set their cannons at newly made embrasures. There then followed a long period of neglect until 1956, when the castle was restored. The parador was installed there in 1965.

That night, the traveler heard talk of the phantom of the fort. On misty mornings in the fall, in December when teams of olive-pickers sing as they work, or in the perfumed nights of summer, the ephemeral ghost of Doña Teresa de Torres, widow of Don Miguel Lucas de Iranzo, *condestable* of Castile, appears on the battlements. On other occasions she is heard playing the *vihuela* (an early form of guitar) and singing the verses of an old song:

Tres Morillas me enamoran en Jaén:
Aixa, Fátima y Marién.
Tres morillas tan garridas
iban a coger olivas
y hallábanlas cogidas en Jaén:
Aixa, Fátima y Marién

(Three Moorish girls beguiled me in Jaén:
Aixa, Fatima and Marién.
Three Moorish girls so fair
went to gather olives
and found them already gathered in Jaén:
Aixa, Fatima and Marién.)

The magnificent interior of the Parador Castillo de Santa Catalina, Jaén. The castle was built by Alfonso X, the Wise, in the mid-13th century. It is named after the former chapel of Santa Catalina, also dating from the 13th century, that was built within one of the towers.

Tapestries and suits of armor displayed in the parador evoke the glories of the past.

Jaén Cathedral seen from the parador. It was completed in the 16th century and is a prime example of the Andalusian Renaissance style. When the city was captured from the Moors in 1245 by Ferdinand III, the Saint, the mosque was temporarily used as a Christian church until work began on the cathedral at the end of the 15th century.

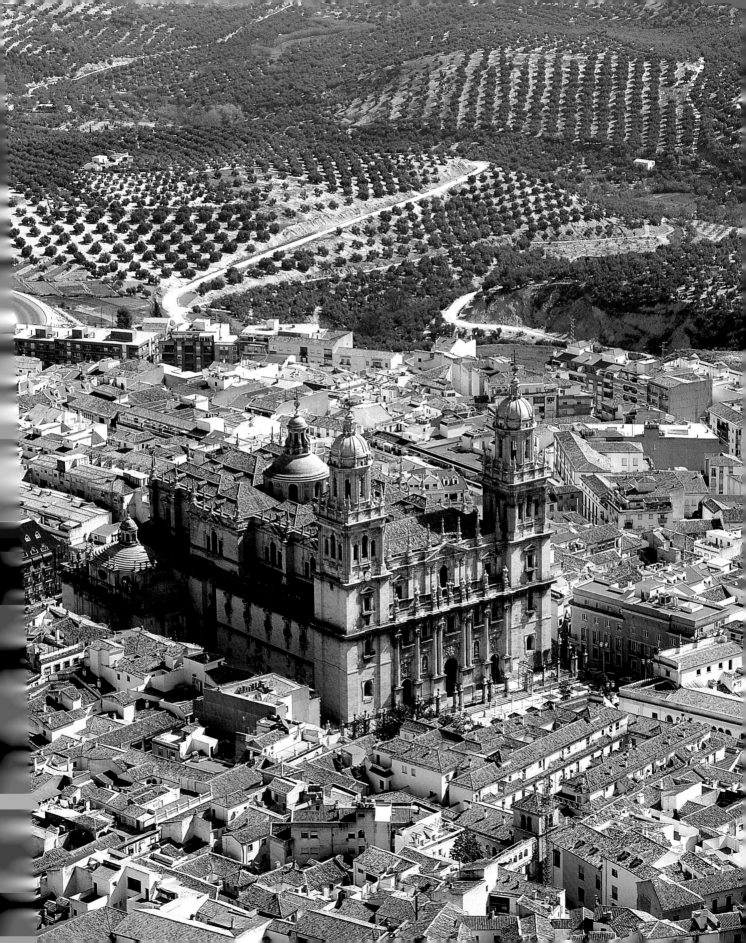

ÚBEDA

«My friend, in the world there are seven city squares: one in Jerusalem, another in Venice, another in Florence, another in Marrakech, another in Castile, and another in Extremadura. The seventh is here, in Úbeda. The rest are just pieces of open ground." The traveler knew all these places and would gladly have added a few more to the list, but with the passing of years he had learnt to agree more and argue less, or disagree less; he readily fell in with the opinions of Don Gualberto Fernández, cloth merchant, and an *Ubedí* proud of his city, also something of an expert on local history.

The Plaza de Vázquez Molina, the square in which the traveler had fallen into conversation with the local scholar, is shaped like an open L, although the uniformity of its design is hidden by rows of trees and small gardens, different kinds of paving, and various other features. The most impressive architectural feature is the chapel of El Salvador. Then there is the palace of Dean Ortega, today the parador of Úbeda, and the palace of Las Cadenas, also known as the Palacio de Vázquez de Molina, which today serves as the city hall. Opposite is an old granary and, at the far end, another Renaissance church, Santa María de los Reales Alcázares; this cloistered church has a spacious interior, with five aisles. It contains many medieval artifacts, and it is here that the soldiers who wrested Úbeda from the Moors and who were rewarded with gifts of land are buried. The other buildings in the square include several palaces.

"And what can you tell me about this parador?"

"You'll probably notice that Úbeda, together with the neighboring town of Baeza, a sort of twin with Úbeda, is the capital of the Renaissance in upper Andalusia. There are so many palaces to see here, built in the 16th century and earlier, that there's no need to go any further to see others. This parador was the residence of the famous Dean Ortega, Don Fernando Ortega Salido, a canon and Dean of Málaga Cathedral.

"Modesty apart, it's Spain's most literary parador: Pío Baroja y Nessi, regarded as the leading Spanish novelist of the 20th century, stayed here shortly after it opened, in 1930, and everybody knows how little Don Pío traveled, which makes it even more remarkable. Hemingway, Lorca, and Jane and Paul Bowles also stayed here."

The Parador de Úbeda was obviously a Moorish palace before it was taken over by the Christians. It may also be that Dean Ortega, who was a man of letters and a lover of the classics, decided to step back in time and give his residence the comfort and

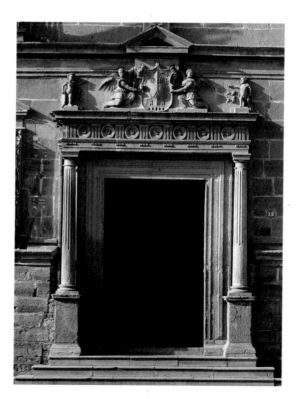

Opposite page: *the entrance to the Parador Condestable Dávalos, in Úbeda.*
Above: *the chapel of San Salvador and the Parador Condestable Dávalos.*

convenience of a Roman palace. The parador has two courtyards: one is paved, with a central fountain and a double arcade of elegant marble columns; the other is an interior courtyard, with wooden balconies and a private garden – it is more secluded and might have been a private area for the women of the house.

As he explored the streets of Úbeda, the traveler paid a visit to the chapel of San Juan de la Cruz, in which are displayed the relics of St John of the Cross and the foreshortened drawing of Christ that inspired Dalí's *Crucifixion*. He also went to Baeza, to see the cathedral, which has close associations with the Romantic poet Antonio Machado y Ruiz, and other places that feature in Machado's poetry. He strolled through the cloisters of the former university and made a foray to the ruins of Cástulo,

ÚBEDA

The Parador de Úbeda is located in a 16th-century palace. Its origins go back to the 15th century, when a palace was built for Don Fernando Ortega Salido, dean of the chapel of El Salvador. This earlier building, remodeled in the 16th century, was designed by Andrés de Vandelvira, the renowned architect of Jaén Cathedral and many other monuments, whose influence spread to the Americas through his pupils. An outstanding feature of the palace is the sober central patio, with a double arcade of columns with elegant capitals. The façade of this two-story building is equally restrained: plain expanses of wall are punctuated by windows with classical pediments.

One of the courtyards in the Parador Condestable Dávalos.

near Linares, the mine that provided Carthage with the silver that financed Hannibal's campaigns. Hannibal married the daughter of the king of Cástulo, a sweet girl named Himilce, who bore him a daughter, Aspar.

The traveler, returning from the gloomy ruins of Cástulo, lunched on a delicious partridge salad seasoned with *ajoblanco* (a kind of mayonnaise made with garlic and olive oil), followed by *suspiros de monja* (nun's sighs), a delicious local confectionery that is not to be confused with the indigestible paste known as *cojoncitos del Señor Abad* (the Abbot's little balls).

The visitor worked off his lunch with a stroll in the parador's courtyard, then went out to the Hospital de los Honrados Viejos del Salvador and climbed to

the top of the old wall. Opposite, beyond a stream and a few fruit trees, began the famous hills of Úbeda.

"Tell me, Don Gualberto, what's all this about wandering the hills of Úbeda?"

"Well, that's the excuse El Cid gave to his lord, Alfonso VI of Castile, when he arrived late at the siege of Úbeda. 'Where the devil have you been, Rodrigo?' demanded the irate king. And El Cid, with his characteristic aplomb replied, 'Wandering these hills, my Lord.'"

The façade of the chapel of El Salvador.
The central scene above the entrance is the
Transfiguration of Christ. Other motifs depict
biblical and secular subjects.

The double-arcaded courtyard at the Parador Condestable Dávalos.

The church of San Pablo was originally a mosque. It is in a mixture of styles, including Romanesque.

ALMAGRO

Anyone who comes to La Mancha and sees the flocks of sheep there or the outline of an occasional windmill will know immediately this is the homeland of Don Quixote. With these thoughts in mind, the traveler proceeded toward Almagro. Beneath a cloudless blue sky, he saw to left and right brown fallow fields, green vineyards, ancient villages with their squares, and beautiful balconies of artistic wrought iron. There was the cool shade of churches; there were humble dwellings with earth-colored or whitewashed walls pierced by tiny windows, from which strings of red peppers had sometimes been hung out to dry in the sun. In the restful ambience of monasteries, the traveler heard the clear toll of the bells that still strike the hours from airy belfries crowned with storks' nests.

The landscape of La Mancha may appear monotonous but for more curious visitors it has unforgettable surprises in store: among these is the maritime museum of La Marina (El Viso del Marqués), curiously located far from the sea; and the flocks of African birds on the Tablas de Daimiel. This is a true ornithologist's paradise, to which a wide variety of birds mysteriously find their way after their journeys over deserts and seas.

Almagro and its surroundings have since ancient times been coveted by a whole succession of peoples. This is as much for its strategic position at a crossroads as for the fertility of the land and richness of its mines; the mercury mine of Almadén, the largest deposit of mercury in the world, has been exploited continuously since Roman times.

During the Crusades, while the kings of Europe fought to snatch the Holy Land back from the Moslems, La Mancha was the setting for a lesser known though equally fierce contest. Like the Knights Templar and the Knights of St John of

Jerusalem in the Holy Land, several orders came to the aid of the king in his military campaigns in Castile. One such, the Order of Calatrava, secured Almagro and the 74 villages in its domain. To this day the Calatrava cross, consisting of four conjoined fleurs-de-lis, is ubiquitous in the region. A few miles from Almagro, guarding the old road from Córdoba to Toledo, stands the largest complex of castles in Europe: these are the fortresses of Calatrava la Vieja, Salvatierra, and Calatrava la Nueva. The latter, which is in fact a monastery, was the seat of the Order of Calatrava and the stronghold where the warrior friars kept their relics and treasures.

Two views of the interior of the Parador de San Francisco, in Almagro.

The bloody battlefields of old are now vineyards where white earth and golden sun combine to produce the revitalising lifeblood of a revered sharp red wine, which serves as a magnificent accompaniment to the regional fare: the delicious *pisto manchego* (a ratatouille of peppers, tomatoes, and other vegetables), roast lamb, game (partridge, hare, or wild boar), and *duelos y quebrantos* (sorrow and affliction – bacon and eggs), a dish that graced Don Quixote's table.

After the fall of the last Moorish kingdom in 1492, the Spanish military orders were absorbed by the Crown. Shortly afterward, in 1519, Charles I of Spain, who had ambitions for the title of Holy Roman Emperor, desperately needed some 1 million florins with which to purchase the support of the main German voters. The German banker and cloth merchant Jacob Fugger came up with the funds and Charles I was elected Holy Roman Emperor (becoming Charles V). In return for the credit that he

had been given, he was forced to lease the fabulous heritage of the military orders to the Fuggers. The Fuggers, like any great lord of La Mancha, built their palace in Almagro, in which they set up their consulate and offices. The business prospered: in the space of a mere 15 years the former Graben cloth merchants had increased fivefold the sum that they had lent the Emperor.

For centuries the mainstay of the economy of La Mancha was the merino sheep, whose wool was much esteemed in the rest of Europe. It was not only the Fuggers who grew rich on the wool trade and cereals markets but also many families and religious orders in Almagro; the ancestral homes, palaces, and monasteries that they built as a result constitute a body of important architectural monuments that together make up the complex of medieval, Renaissance, and Baroque buildings that is Almagro. Even the humble Franciscans lived in a magnificent monastery, now the Parador de San Francisco, built

ALMAGRO

The parador is located in the former monastery of San Francisco, built in 1596 by Don Jerónimo Dávila. The city was inhabited successively by Romans, Visigoths, and Moors, and grew in importance as it was repopulated by Christians after the Battle of Navas de Tolosa in 1212. Shortly afterward the Order of Calatrava was founded, with its seat in Almagro, capital of the large province of La Mancha.

in 1596. So vast is the building, with 14 patios and numberless galleries, lobbies, chapels, cells, cellars, granaries, and workshops, that it is difficult to believe that it was ever completely occupied. Life there, in the present-day parador, is certainly more relaxed than it was when the building was a monastery. Franciscan regulations required that the friars gather in church to say their prayers (*Maitines* and *Parvo*) from midnight until 3am, and then again at daybreak.

In Almagro the monasteries, churches, palaces, and mansions of rich citizens are enclosed private worlds. By contrast, the Plaza Mayor, in the center of this prosperous city, is the town's focal point and proclaims the wellbeing of Almagro's citizens. The square, one of the finest in the world, is a wide, open rectangular space lined on its longer sides by a uniform row of old houses supported on arcades of

The traveler in La Mancha will inevitably fall to thinking about Don Quixote running the wineskins through. The bloody battlefields of old are today vineyards that produce an abundance of wine.

Following pages:
Three views of the Plaza Mayor in Almagro.

The Corral de Comedias in Almagro. It was thanks to this famous theater that plays by Cervantes, Lope de Vega, and others – classics of the Spanish Golden Age – became known in the 16th century.

stone columns. In the green-painted windows hang embroidered curtains, while in spaces opened in the walls beneath the roof, strings of sausages and vegetables, bunches of grapes, and melons can be glimpsed hanging up from the rafters to dry – well-kept pantries that reflect the comfortable living enjoyed by these householders.

On one side of the square stands the Corral de Comedias, the oldest theater in Europe, which dates back to the time of Cervantes and Shakespeare. In its galleries and stalls, in its backstage dressing rooms, the visitor can imagine the hullabaloo of the *mosqueteros* (male members of the audience who stood in the patio) and the bustle of cushions and stools in the upper galleries, which were reserved for women and noble families, and the privileged spectators who sat in folding chairs on the stage itself.

ALARCÓN

A round 1200 years ago, a Visigothic prince out hunting wild boar in the rugged oak woods of Castile came upon a mountain that was almost completely surrounded by a river. Only a short isthmus prevented it from being an island, with a heart-shaped outline. When he returned to Toledo, the prince described the mountain to his father, King Alaric, and persuaded him to a build a fortress there. The fortress would bear his name: Alaricón.

It was in pursuit of a legend that the traveler had come to Alarcón, but he found much more. It was a bright sunny morning and a migrating stork flew by to his right, its destination the belfries of La Mancha; the traveler, who had read the *Poema del Mío Sid*, took this to be a good omen. About a mile from

ALARCÓN

Alarcón is an impressive medieval town set on an outcrop of rock, its castle perching on the highest point. In 785 Mohammed el Fehari, son of the deposed king of Toledo, sought refuge here, feigning blindness. After he had conquered Cuenca in 1117, Alfonso VIII set his army on Alarcón. He laid siege to the town for nine months, and was victorious when, scaling the walls by means of two daggers, his knight Hernán Martínez de Cevallos reached the battlements and penetrated the town. In recognition of this daring feat, the king granted him permission to change his surname to Alarcón.

Previous page and opposite page: *the castle at Alarcón.*
Above: *a well in a peaceful courtyard in Alarcón.*

Alarcón, mostly to postpone the pleasure of his arrival, he parked his car at a vantage point from which it was possible to see Alarcón and the famous bend in the Júcar that embraces the town. From this distance he contemplated the medieval town. There was the castle, set on the crest of the mountain, its keep crowned by battlements and machicolations. Around the keep is the impregnable *alcazarejo* (citadel). The horizontal plane of its long windowless walls is offset by tall corner towers. The *alcazarejo* is in turn enclosed within concentric walls set with turrets overlooking the scarp; these walls encircle the town and resemble a golden bracelet that the sun has polished brightly with the patience of centuries. Rising from the waters of the Júcar, luxuriant vegetation scrambles over scarps and ravines, hanging from the walls and covering the outcrop of rock. That vibrant green adds a verdant strain to complete this landscape of ochers and the blues of the limpid sky.

Rows of walls set with turrets surround Alarcón like a golden bracelet burnished by the sun. The castle was the scene of many feats of arms during the Middle Ages; it was here that the Marquis of Villena was besieged by Jorge Manrique and Pedro Ruiz de Alarcón.

The traveler noticed a curious feature: on one side the city wall was extended to run right down the hillside as far as the river, stopping right there at the bank. Later, in the lounge of the parador at Alarcón, Don Federico de Villena, an authority on castles, explained:

"What you're talking about is the *coracha*. These walls that run right down to the water's edge generally end with a hollow tower with a well inside it. This was so that the defenders of the castle had safe access to a water supply. Almost all the castles and walled cities that fell after a long siege did so because the water ran out. That is why it was crucial to have protected access to the nearest river or well."

The following day, after a hearty breakfast, Don Federico de Villena accompanied the traveler on his tour of the town and its defenses.

"These walls and these towers have witnessed the whole of Spain's history. Imagine: after the kingdom of the Visigoths had been destroyed by the Moors in 711, the castle entered a dark period of neglect, possibly because it was not close to any frontier. But when Moorish Spain split up into a dozen or so petty kingdoms, Alarcón regained its importance, being strategically placed on the border of one of these kingdoms, Toledo."

In 1184 Alfonso VIII, king of Castile, conquered the Cuenca, taking the region city by city, village by village, fortress by fortress. Alarcón fell thanks to the daring of one of Alfonso's knights: taking advantage of a starless night, he scaled the city walls by sticking his two daggers into the slits between the stones, penetrated the town, slew the sentries and, like Ulysses at the siege of Troy, allowed the besieging forces to break through. The knight, one Hernán Martínez de Cevallos, changed his name to Alarcón in memory of the feat.

The king of Castile, now finally master of the area, set diligently about repopulating it by assigning

This 16th-century palace is now the town hall.

fueros (statutes) that granted substantial fiscal and legal concessions to those willing to participate in the plan. It was not long before the chimneys of Alarcón were smoking again and peasant farmers and shepherds once more walked the streets. The proximity of the kingdom's frontiers, and the city's strategic position on the borders of the Meseta and the Levante, lay the area open to great danger. The *fuero* stipulated that landowners should work with an armed escort during the potentially more perilous months: "herders must be escorted by one horseman for every two herds of cows or three of sheep… and the horseman must be mounted on a horse worth over 20 *maravediés*."

Back from their morning walk along the walls overlooking the cleft and the fertile Júcar plain, the two friends strolled along the Calle Meastra, which runs the whole length of the medieval town and opens out onto a spacious square: on one side of the square is a 16th-century palace, now the town hall, on another the so-called palace house, a magnificent vernacular Baroque building, and on another the church of St John the Baptist, with its fine Mannerist doorway. The traveler saw from an inscription that this was the Plaza de Don Juan Manuel.

"Don Juan Manuel," said Don Federico, "was a grandee of the sword and of letters, the grandson and nephew of kings. He was so precocious that he fought in his first battle at the age of 12. In adulthood he took part in the famous siege of Algeciras, fighting alongside knights from all over Europe. He married, and was left a widower, three times; his wives were either princesses or ladies of noble birth. When he tired of the world he turned to reading and writing, and withdrew to the monastery of Peñafiel, where he died. He was the father of the Spanish novel, the author of *El Conde Lucanor* (*Count Lucanor*), published in 1335, a pleasant collection of short stories of an ingenuity comparable to that of Boccaccio, except that he wrote them 13 years earlier than the *Decameron*. One, about the 'Young Man who Married a Wild, Strong-Willed Woman,' was the inspiration for Shakespeare's *Taming of the Shrew*."

The traveler and his host lunched hungrily, feasting on *morteruelo*, a local pâté made of several different meats, in a dining room adorned with the standards of the knights who conquered Alarcón and became grandees of the city. Later they took coffee in the lounge of the parador, a room with tapestries, heavy chairs and other medieval furnishings.

CUENCA

The traveler had heard much about Cuenca: its houses, clinging to an outcrop of rock, give Cuenca, built upon stone but seeming to hang in the air, the peculiar quality of a city that looks as if it might take flight. However, as he reached the city, raising his eyes from the defile of the Huécar, whose limpid waters have for thousands of years been slowly carving out that impressive gorge, the newcomer could only marvel at the fact that a city could have been built in such a precarious location. Don Federico de Villena had already given him some background information:

"Like many Spanish towns and cities, Cuenca is a consequence of the long-drawn-out travails of the Reconquista. The people who chose to make a town here did so thinking more in terms of defense than of the comfort of its inhabitants. Here was a high, narrow, rocky plateau encircled by two deep gorges each gouged out by a river, the Júcar and the Huécar, and they didn't think twice about colonizing it. A more strategically advantageous place would have been impossible to find; it was like a Castilian advance post on the Levantine flank, open to the sea."

Opposite page: *Cuenca.*
Above: *the cloister of the parador at Cuenca, originally a 17th-century Dominican monastery.*

Memories of the old Dominican monastery still pervade the rooms and corridors of the Parador de San Pablo.

Right: *the gorge of the Huécar river viewed from the Parador de San Pablo.*

All this took place in the 8th century. The Moors, who founded Cuenca, built a castle at the highest point. As time went by, a cluster of humble shacks, and later relatively solid houses, began to grow up around the castle. When Alfonso VIII of Castile conquered the town in 1117, Cuenca had become a city.

Following the defile of the Huécar, the traveler found the Parador de San Pablo without difficulty and parked opposite the church, with its arresting Churrigueresque Baroque façade. Through the empty belfry he caught sight of clouds, like lumps of cotton wool, scudding across the sky.

As he walked through the rooms, corridors, and chapels of the parador, originally a monastery, the traveler, by nature observant, could not help noticing a curious detail.

CUENCA

The parador is housed in the former monastery of San Pablo. It was built by Father Juan del Pozo, who dedicated it in 1523. The monastery, a fine example of 16th-century Gothic architecture, stands on a promontory overlooking the Huécar, one of the rivers that encircle Cuenca. From this vantage point you can view the center of the town, the Casas Colgadas (Hanging Houses) and the great Anglo-Norman cathedral. This historically important complex, including the monastery of San Pablo (now the parador), was recently declared a World Heritage Site by UNESCO.

The cloister of the Parador de San Pablo,
Cuenca, formerly a Dominican monastery.

"Excuse me, but apart from the Dominican coat of arms I keep seeing these letters. They're repeated all over the building. What do they mean?"

"That's the anagram of the monastery's founder, Juan del Pozo Pino, canon of Cuenca Cathedral, who, according to hearsay, had a slave who was black and mute; black because he'd been born in Africa and mute because he'd had his tongue cut out. He wasn't deaf, though, and one night, seeing that thieves had stolen his master's coffer, in which he kept various bags full of gold pieces, he sounded the alarm and, even though it was foggy, followed the thieves' tracks as far as a rocky place on the Huécar called La Sultana, a bare outcrop surrounded by the escarpments of the cleft. Thanks to him, the party that had gone out in pursuit of the robbers finally caught them and recovered the treasure. The canon took this as a sign from heaven and spent his fortune on founding the monastery on that same rock."

"But there's no precipice here."

"Not on this side, you mean. If you wanted to leave by the other side you'd have to fly, because there's a drop as sharp as the one under the hanging houses."

The parador in Cuenca has 14 sections of roof and a cloistered courtyard with a fountain and two tall, dark cypresses. The traveler was given a room (which was originally a cell) on the side of the monastery overlooking the precipice; from there, looking up to the neighboring flat-topped hillock, he saw the castle, built by the Moors and captured by the Christians, in which the first prison of the Inquisition was made.

To reach the city, the traveler took the iron catwalk across the Huécar gorge, climbed a rocky slope, then passed through a gateway of sturdy cantilevered beams that marks the entrance to Cuenca. After wandering for a while along twisting stone-paved streets, he soon came to the Plaza de Ronda. There he sat on a stone and turned his mind to deciphering the inscription on the rear façade of the archeological museum: *Omnia opera mortalia mortalitate damnata sunt. Inter peritura vivimus*, which he translated as "Every human enterprise

is condemned to death. We live among things perishable."

As he wandered through the medieval city, the traveler saw tiny gardens and orchards clinging to the precipice, and noted various small details of the beautiful old city – wrought ironwork, fountains, walled private gardens and lofty belvederes, tiny market gardens overlooking the abyss. All this seemed to him to be the result of a symbiosis between human settlement and natural rock that had been extended to make walls, ledges that turned into escarpments, and houses that climbed chaotically on top of other houses in a confused jumble of architecture. From a belvedere the traveler looked down to the winding river below, lined with trees that glistened with every shade of green and yellow.

Seen from a distance, Cuenca seems lost in a vast landscape. For some the city is mysterious and almost a place of pilgrimage.

Cuenca Cathedral, which Alfonso VIII built on the site of the old mosque.

A magical sunset behind the Casas Colgadas (Hanging Houses) at Cuenca. They built in the 15th century and today house the Museo de Arte Abstracto Español.

As he toured the cathedral, the traveler thought that Cuenca is a mysterious city, a city of the Holy Grail (as its heraldry proclaims), an enclave where the forces of the earth meet those of the air.

He returned to his lodgings by the iron bridge over the gorge. It was midday, and he lunched ravenously in the old refectory under the shadow of a built-in pulpit; from there, in the days when the parador was a monastery, a reader would entertain the silent eaters with passages from the Bible. The first course, a salad of artichokes and spinach, seemed to him to epitomise the very essence of vegetables that could hardly be bettered; but the part of the meal that most pleased him was the local dessert, an *alajú* tart, made with bread, walnuts, and honey, which he washed down with two small glasses of *resolí* liqueur.

"And this liqueur, what is it made from?"

"It was invented as a cure for nostalgia by a friar who had been a sailor, and possibly a pirate, on the distant sea routes of the spice trade. This is why the ingredients for such a landlocked recipe include so many delights from overseas: coffee, cinnamon, orange peel, and sugar."

That afternoon, the traveler returned to the city, and once again became lost in the maze of old streets. Sitting on the railings of a small vegetable garden, he watched a group of nuns go past. One of them, whose shrill voice betrayed nerves slightly on edge proclaimed: "When I have to pray I think of places like this, which I have enjoyed. It helps me concentrate."

That night, the traveler slept soundly in his cell, soothed by the distant murmur of the Huécar.

CHINCHÓN

Chinchón is a town of valiant and hospitable people. In 1808, in the wake of the popular uprising against Napoleonic troops, a French reconnoitering patrol made so bold as to venture as far as the main square, next to the parador where the traveler was now staying. "Two members of the patrol were shot dead," according to an account at the time, "and another two were stoned to death."

In the main square, as he saw the monument known as the Columna de los Franceses (Frenchmen's Column), the traveler reflected on whether the townspeople of Chinchón got their mettle from anisette; they had after all shown themselves capable of getting rid of a French monster who had been victorious at the Battle of Austerlitz.

"Then everything went wrong. More French troops arrived, the townspeople were outnumbered, and Chinchón was razed to the ground."

Besides being valiant and hospitable, the people of Chinchón are admirably skilled in the kitchen, and their roasts are so famed that *Madrileños* come to their restaurants whenever they have something to celebrate; some people even contrive business trips just to be able to stop for lunch in Chinchón. And after the roast and the rice pudding comes a glass of Chinchón anisette.

As he was a stranger, the traveler did not know about Chinchón anisette:

A native put him wise: "Chinchón is an aniseed-flavored spirit, sweet or dry, made by distilling green aniseed in a mixture of natural alcohols in copper stills."

The Chinchón anisette is fêted as the best in Spain, and it is very good taken on the rocks after dessert. This is wise alchemy; it reduces its strength and turns it from translucent to white, hence the name *palomita* (little dove).

In the 17th century, the parador where the traveler was staying had been the Augustinian monastery of Santa María del Paraíso. The monks had established their own university there; there were various departments, and they taught humanities, theology, and Latin. This went on until the 19th century, when the government seized the monastery and converted it into law courts and a jail. From then circumstances for the monastery went from bad to worse, reaching a nadir in 1929, when it was destroyed by fire. All that remained was the Chapel of the Rosary and the main staircase, with its beautiful, picturesque frescoes and ornamentation. Being sufficiently robust, and of good masonry and brickwork, the monastery walls also survived the fire, leaving a shell in which the present-day parador was built. As he walked round the cloisters and rooms of the former monastery, the traveler marveled at the fact that all that he saw had been so faithfully

The courtyard of the parador in Chinchón, where the coolness of the water is as welcome as the renowned local anisette.

The monastery of Santa María del Paraíso was also a center of learning, where the humanities, theology, and Latin were taught.

restored and saved from certain ruin. The figures of saints and of the Virgin Mary that form the subject matter of paintings and wall hangings and the motifs of decorative tiles are a reminder of the building's religious origins, as is the ancient still that stands in a corner of the parador.

The traveler also saw a painting depicting Doña Ana de Osorio, countess of Chinchón and wife of the viceroy of Peru, the first person to bring quinine back from the Americas. It is because of this that the eminent Swedish naturalist Carolus Linnaeus gave it the name *chinchona*.

CHINCHÓN

The parador stands in a former Augustinian monastery founded late in the 15th century by the marquises of Moya, the first lords of Chinchón. The most interesting part of the complex is the church with its rib-vaulted ceiling pierced by lunettes and dome. The pendentives feature the coats of arms of the Cabrera-Bobadilla family, the surnames of the first Marquis of Chinchón and his wife, respectively.

Top: *The figures of saints and of the Virgin Mary that form the subject matter of paintings and
wall hangings and the motifs of decorative tiles are a reminder of the building's religious origins.*
Above: *the cloisters and rooms are redolent of the days when Doña Ana de Osorio, Countess of Chinchón and wife of the viceroy of
Peru, frequented these premises. Although severely damaged by fire in 1929, the building has been restored to its original appearance.*

The central staircase was built into the space where the chapel of La Soledad, founded in 1665 once stood.

The interior of the building is decorated with frescoes and painted tiles.

The lounge of the parador at Chinchón.

The Plaza Mayo, Chinchón. With its multiple wooden galleries, it is a typical Castilian arcaded square.

The garden around the entrance to the parador at Chinchón.

The castle at Chinchón was built in the 15th century. It has a rectangular ground plan, corner towers, and a deep moat.

ÁVILA

In the gardens of the parador, the visitor sat on a bench in the shade of St Teresa's mulberry tree.

"Why is it called St Teresa's mulberry tree?"

"Because it was this ancient tree that the saint used to climb when she was a little girl, or a tomboy more likely, to pick mulberries. The palace then belonged to the Benavides family, the matriarch of which was a relation of the saint's mother."

The traveler, who in matters of Spain would fall back on the opinions of Miguel de Unamuno, the contradictory man of letters, recalled the following words from his pen: "*Lo mejor de España es Castilla. Y en Castilla pocas ciudades, si es que hay alguna, superior a Ávila.*" (Castile is the best part of Spain. And in Castile few cities, if any, are finer than Ávila.)

In the peace of the garden, disturbed only by the

A painting of St Teresa hangs in one of the rooms of the parador.

Above and right: *the courtyard of the parador, now enclosed
by glass.*

chattering of birds in the trees and flower beds, the
traveler took in the medieval city walls, made of
massive blocks of stone, and the Puerta del Carmen,
one of the eight city gates; as he did so he thought of
the harsh lives of the original inhabitants of Ávila,
descendants of the conquerors of the desert plains of
the Duero, who dwelt in a no-man's-land between
Moors and Christians and who, from the 9th century,
held it for Castile. He thought also, recalling
St Teresa's valiant girlhood, that the proximity of war
must have produced some extremely tough women;
from these very walls, their hair gathered up beneath
the hats of their absent brothers and husbands,
women had put to flight Moors who had attempted
to seize the apparently defenseless city.

"In memory of this, the city's coat of arms
features five hats."

The palace of Piedras Albas, in Avila, now a parador.

The traveler climbed the steps leading up to the sentry walk and passed from tower to tower until he reached the crenelated terrace and the fortifications that defend the Puerta del Carmen. From this great viewpoint, he looked out across fields that seemed to be spattered with small, flat outcrops of granite poking up here and there in the grass and along paths. Then, turning back toward the city, he looked at the red roofs and brown walls of the parador, the old Benavides palace. The massive stone tower, around which the other parts of the palace are clustered, show that its builders obviously had military intentions. With the passing of the centuries, however, the interior has taken on a more comfortable, domestic character, though the characteristically Castilian austerity survives in the large halls, sunlit rooms, and a courtyard lined with an elegant granite arcade. The traveler's attention was caught by a typically Castilian method

ÁVILA

The parador is named after Raimundo de Borgoña in memory of the count of Burgundy, son-in-law of Alfonso VI, who conquered the city and fortified it with its famous walls between 1088 and 1099. The parador is located in the 15th-century palace of Piedras Albas, so called after the characteristic white color of the stone from which it is built. It was later substantially altered, but it has always held a prominent place among the many ancestral homes in Ávila, the "city of gentlemen."

Ávila is encircled by about 1½ miles of defensive walls. They were begun in about 1091 by Raimundo de Borgoña
Opposite page: *the storks of Ávila also have their strategic vantage point.*

of construction: the robust walls were made of alternating solid brick and pisé.

"Are these blocks of material between the brickwork really nothing more than packed earth?"

"They certainly are: solid trodden earth. This material maintains an even temperature inside, providing insulation from the cold in winter and from the searing heat in summer."

The former occupants of the palace, who valued the pen as well as the sword, put together a library of around 35,000 volumes specializing in subjects relating to St Teresa, Cervantes, and bullfighting.

Strolling through the city, the traveler divided his time between the cathedral, the churches, and the monastery of La Encarnación; it was here, in one of the cells, that Teresa meditated and occasionally miraculously levitated, and that the community chaplain, Juan de la Cruz, Spain's most exalted poet, burned in the love of God. Teresa herself wrote:

"It is impossible to talk about God with Brother Juan because both he and his listeners become transported."

The traveler also visited the tomb of Prince Juan, the first child of the Catholic Kings, who died of love, that is, of excessive sexual intercourse with his wife, the insatiable Margaret of Burgundy. After his death the Spanish Crown eventually passed to Margaret's brother, Philip the Good; thus was Spain introduced to the Habsburg dynasty, who for centuries inflicted upon the country an absurd policy of wars and squandering. The traveler reflected how youthful passion could change the course of history.

On another day, before leaving the city, the traveler bought a box of *yemas de Santa Teresa* (soft sweets made with egg-yolk), another of *bocaditos de San Honorato*, and another of *rosquillas* (both of them a kind of donut), all highly prized local delicacies.

SIGÜENZA

No one can come away from Sigüenza without having paid a visit to the *doncel* (young nobleman). His name was Martín Vázquez de Arce and he was killed in 1486 on the Acequia Gorda, near Granada, during a skirmish with the Moors. This was at the time when the last bastion of Moorish power in Spain was about to be toppled by the Catholic Kings.

A white marble effigy of the *doncel* lies upon his tomb. He is shown in a full suit of armor, the breastplate with the cross of St James painted in red, indicating his status (he was a Knight Commander of the Order of St James), and he holds in his hands an open book. Isabella of Castile commissioned the sculpture from one Master Juan, who produced what is perhaps the most moving tomb effigy of its kind in the world. The traveler would have given anything to know what book the *doncel* was reading. Perhaps it was a book of poems by his contemporary, Jorge Manrique, another valiant knight who died with his sword in his hand, and whose poetry speaks of the life of fame that awaits the knight when he departs this world of deceit and flattery.

Although dead for five centuries, the doncel of

Sigüenza still acts like a magnet to women. Schoolgirls on end-of-year trips invade the chapel and gather to sigh around his tomb.

The traveler then went on looking round the cathedral fortress, built in a Romanesque-Gothic style. As he paced the aisles adorned with ornate tombs, he recalled Garcilaso de la Vega, José de Cadalso, and other Spanish military men who, like the *doncel* and Jorge Manrique, were men of letters as well as of the sword; so too were Cervantes and Lope de Vega. In the sacristy he came upon the altar-tomb of Santa Librada. In the Middle Ages, Santa Librada was the patron of whores. By extension, she is also the patron saint of women in labor. According to certain sources, pregnant women would come to Sigüenza Cathedral and recite this prayer:

Santa Librada	(Santa Librada
Santa Librada	Santa Librada
que la salida	may the way out
sea tan dulce	be as sweet
como la entrada	as the way in)

The traveler had intended to continue his journey but, having visited the cathedral and taken a walk through the town, which he found equally beautiful, he changed his plans and decided to stay the night. The parador of Sigüenza is set on a hill overlooking the town. Its history is a compendium of the history of Spain, for Romans, Goths, and Moors had settled here before Bishop Bernardo de Agén built a castle-residence in 1124. The bishop's successors gradually extended the castle, transforming it into a palatial residence rather than a fortified palace. The building contains many interesting and beautiful features, and the visitor saw them all: among them are the 16th-century Torres Gemelas (Twin Towers), the throne room with two fine French fireplaces and a magnificent wood-

Opposite page: *the courtyard of the medieval castle of Sigüenza, now a parador.*
Above: *the Torres Gemelas, the 16th-century castle gatehouse.*
Left: *an interior view of the parador.*

beamed ceiling supported on mighty pillars, the Romanesque chapel, the large paved courtyard with its central well, and the Torres de las Campanas (Bell Towers). Everywhere he looked were suits of armor, helmets, and standards. Having reached the dining room, in the Torre de Doña Blanca, he lunched on roast kid followed by *bizcochos borrachos* (sponge fingers in liqueur sauce) as a tribute to the Nobel Prize-winner Camilo José Cela, who recommends them highly in his Nuevo Viaje a Alcarria.

Below: *the Salón del Trono, with its elegant French fireplaces and ceiling beams.*

Opposite page: *the dining room.*
Following pages: *bare stone, terracotta tiling, and ceiling beams make an attractive combination.*

SIGÜENZA

The foundations of the medieval castle that now houses the parador rest on earlier Iberian, Roman, Visigothic, and Moorish settlements. After it had been retaken from the Moors in 1124, it became the residence of Bishop Bernardo de Agén. The building was substantially remodeled in the 14th century by Bishop Simón Girón de Cisneros and by Cardinal Fonserca in the 15th. Its most outstanding room is the Salón del Trono, featuring two French-style fireplaces.

Two views of the chapel.

ques de arse comendador desant yño elqual fue muerte
n de framela miercoles mes del marçe

Taking a last look at the parador standing on the hilltop is as much of a ritual as buying the local delicacies: the soft sweets known as yemas de Santa Teresa and donuts known as bocaditos de San Honorato.

Sigüenza Cathedral, a fortified church, was built between the 12th and the 15th centuries.

Previous pages: the Gothic tomb effigy of the doncel *of Sigüenza, a young knight named Martín Vázquez de Arce, who was slain on the plain of Granada while fighting to expel the Moors. The sculpture, which dates from the 15th century, is by Master Juan.*

CARDONA

Strabo, the Greek geographer who lived shortly before the time of Christ, and Aulus Gellius, the 2nd-century Roman writer, both extolled as a wonder of nature the Cardona salt deposit: it was "a great mountain of pure salt that grows as it is extracted." The Romans had good reason to believe that the salt grew, since they excavated whole galleries down to depths never before reached and all they found was salt and still more salt. The traveler, curious by nature, spent a whole morning visiting that petrified blue sea that the local people imaginatively christened La Salina (The Salt Mine). Penetrating the depths of the mine he reached underground lakes and admired the fantastic natural shapes of the stalactites of salt in the grottos.

"And you say that this deposit never diminishes in size."

"Well, it has to diminish, of course, but there's enough salt here to cure more hams than anybody could eat in the next thousand generations: experts reckon it amounts to 500 billion tons."

Landlocked Cardona, on the border between the provinces of Barcelona and Lérida, with the Pyrenean foothills rising up on the clear horizon, has other associations with the sea besides salt. In the early 9th century, the town belonged to Don Ramon Folch, duke of Cardona, grand admiral and grand *condestable* of Aragon. Aragon was not yet the master of the Mediterranean that it was to become several centuries later; by the early Middle Ages its proud motto was "even the fish must sport the stripes of Aragon." Later, one of the first duke of Cardona's descendants, another Admiral Ramon

From the highest points of the hill,
watchtowers look out over the plain.

*The Parador Duques de Cardona. The castle at Cardona, built in the mid-9th century,
has lost nothing of its majestic medieval appearance.*

The crypt beneath the central nave of the collegiate church of San Vicente.

Folch, played a leading role on land and sea in the conquest of Naples for Ferdinand the Catholic. He had a reputation for cruelty in war and cunning in negotiation. A great warlord, he is buried in Bellpuig in a magnificent Renaissance tomb.

Cardona stands on a hill overlooking the plain of the river Cardoner. From a distance it looks solid and majestic, its three concentric walls and its bastions seeming to wrap themselves round the hill to culminate in two contrasting buildings: on one side the vertical walls of the collegiate church of San Vicente and on the other the massive cone of the castle keep, impressive despite its truncated top. Dating from the 11th century, it is one of the oldest keeps in Europe.

The Torre Minyona is associated with a legend.

In the 11th century, the daughter of the first viscount of the area fell in love with the *alcaide* (Moorish governor) of a nearby castle. The Moor, thoroughly lovestruck, agreed to renounce the Koran, but the lords of the castle still refused to accept him as a son-in-law. Since the young girl would not relinquish her love for the Moor, she was walled up inside the Torre Minyona with no contact with the outside world other than a dumb servant who brought her her meals every day. She remained firm in her resolve, however, and preferred to die in captivity rather than succumb to family pressures. It might be the girl's ghost that sometimes haunts room 712 of the parador. She must be a lovelorn, sorrowful, and peaceful ghost, though for all she does is open doors and windows, as discreetly as possible so as not to disturb anyone.

CARDONA

In 798, Louis of Aquitaine, Charlemagne's successor, ordered that Cardona be populated and restored. The revolts of Aissó and al-Mansur resulted in the flight of the local population, a situation that was not reversed until 986, when Borrell II repopulated the area.

In the 10th century the viscounts of Osona settled in the fortress, which fell within the county of Barcelona, and founded the distinguished Cardona dynasty, which persisted until the late 17th century. The most important building in Cardona is the Romanesque church of San Vicente, consecrated in 1040. Also noteworthy is the Torre de la Minyona, the ancient keep with its tragic legend, and former refectory of the original monastery, which today is the dining room of the parador.

In Cardona, the traveler was irresistibly drawn to those places that seem to breathe history. As he explored the labyrinth of narrow streets created by the haphazard accumulation of buildings, he found that it was but a short walk from the Romanesque collegiate church, with its nave flanked by aisles and the serried ranks of tombs of the counts and dukes of Cardona, to the 11th-century church built on the site of a Roman courtyard and, a little further on, to the 15th-century Gothic cloister.

Returning to the castle gate, via the Tower of San Pedro and the Devil's Sentry Box (unexpected and evocative names), he reverently entered the small room, today a chapel, in which in 1240 died St Ramón Nonato, a member of the ducal family of Cardona.

"If he was a Cardona, why do they call him Nonato – the Unborn?"

"Because he was born by Cesarean section after his mother had died, and this was seen as a miracle. That's why he's the patron saint of expectant mothers and on his feast day, August 31, pregnant women

Cardona is a town that seems to breathe history.

traditionally walk round his shrine three times – it's on the road to Berga – to ensure that their labor will be over quickly."

That night, after a meal of *escudella* (a typical Catalan noodle stew) and kid cooked Berga-style, taken in the huge vaulted dining hall, the traveler headed for bed with the aftertaste of *crema catalana* and Penedès wine still playing on his palate. He fell sound asleep, soothed by the deep silences of the plain and the harmony of the night sky.

The following day he had no need to get up early, because he wanted to reach Montserrat, site of the famous monastery, some 80 miles from Cardona, at midday. Although his taste was for Mozart rather than Wagner, the traveler wanted to visit the mountain that inspired Parsifal and of which Goethe wrote: "in no other part of the world will anyone find the peace and happiness of Montserrat."

Above, right, and following pages: *the collegiate church of San Vicente, a fine example of early Romanesque style in Catalonia. The nave is flanked by aisles, and each terminates in an apse. The wide transept is crowned by a central dome.*

Opposite page: *the salt mines at Cardona.*

Above: *a panoramic view of the town.*

TORTOSA

The castle of La Zuda has been the seat of three kings who have played a pivotal roles in the history of Spain: Abd-ar-Rahman III, who in 944 ordered the well (*zuda* – after which the castle is named) to be made; Count Ramon Berenguer IV, who reclaimed Tortosa from the Moors in 1148, and James I of Aragon. It subsequently came into the hands of the Knights Templar.

The traveler had entered the city through the horseshoe arch at the main gates. Looking out from the window of his room, he thought about all the history that was contained within those walls. He watched the sun rise over the plain of the Ebro, where at its spectacular delta the river floods marshlands and rice plantations.

The traveler imagined that Abd-ar-Rahman, at the height of his glory – having victoriously subdued all the Christian kingdoms on the Iberian peninsula –

might have watched from this very window the approach of the ambassador of Byzantium, or of France or Germany, or of one of the Italian city states at a time when, at the zenith of his power, the whole of Christendom competed for his friendship. According to Ben Idhari, Abd-ar-Rahman was "fair-skinned, with deep blue eyes; of medium height, well proportioned and elegant; he dyed his skin black." The traveler reflected that he might have dyed his skin black to please his Cordoban lover, and it was perhaps the infinitely wide landscape of La Zuda that inspired his innermost soul to write these nostalgic lines:

> *Hoy, ausente de mi amada, experimento penas sin remedio*
> *La rosa acrecienta mi tristeza, la azucena no me da reposo*
> *Mis noches antes deliciosas me parecen feas como rostros deformes*
> *Nada esperes de lo que deseas, ni que los cuidados te dejen.*

Today, without my love, I feel incurable sorrow
The rose increases my sorrow, the lily gives me no repose
My nights, once delicious, now seem as ugly as deformed faces
Expect nothing from what you desire, nor that your cares ever will leave you.

Ramon Berenguer IV, king of Aragon and count of Barcelona, won the castle back from the Moors and kept his powerful enemies at bay on this and the other side of the Pyrenees. He also conquered the Levant and died in a village in Piedmont, Italy, at the age of 47.

TORTOSA

The castle stands on a hill beneath which flows the wide river Ebro, an important landmark since ancient times. The Iberian hill fort that once stood here was extended by the Romans and in 714 by the Moors, shortly after their arrival in Europe. Reconquered by Count Ramon Berenguer IV in 1148, the fortress was a royal residence during the reign of James I of Aragon and, simultaneously, the city became a see: the fine Catalan Gothic cathedral can be seen from the castle. The fortress was also a royal dungeon and, for a time, belonged to the Knights Templar.

Tortosa at dusk. The Castillo de la Zuda that crowns the hill, and where the parador is located, stands on the site of a prehistoric Iberian settlement. It later became a Roman stronghold.

James I of Aragon was the third conqueror to drink the waters of La Zuda, and from his rooms in the Torre Punta del Diamante he dreamed of faraway lands as he looked out over the immense plains of the delta. From this castle he planned the conquests of Morella and Peñíscola, which would open the land route to Valencia. Having contemplated the conquest of the lands assigned to his kingdom, he still had energy and generosity enough to aid Castile in the conquest of Murcia and to send a crusade to the Holy Land. All that he failed to conquer were his sons, by two different marriages, who on his death would contest the throne.

During the reign of Alfonso II, the Chaste, the Knights Templar took an active part in expeditions against Mertín, Alhambra, and Caspe. As a reward for their services they were given a third of Tortosa and a fifth of Lérida. Guillén de Monredón, master of the Knights Templar in Aragon, aided James I during the latter's minority and subsequently helped him conquer Mallorca and Valencia. When came the terrible day that the order of the Knights Templar was supressed, the Templars refused to surrender and shut themselves inside their fortresses. Lacking aid from outside, Templar castles in Aragon fell one by one. However, unlike their French counterparts, the defenders did not die at the stake because the Council of Tarragona declared them innocent. La Zuda escaped that tragic episode because, in 1294, some years before the purge against the Templars, James II of Castile had acquired the town from the order, along with other castles in the region, in exchange for Peñíscola and other cities.

Having lunched on the renowned seafood of the region, the traveler strolled along the sentry walk to the artillery bastion, which commands a view over the roofs of the Gothic cathedral. Then he visited the cathedral, and the nave and altarpiece of which he had heard so much.

Previous pages: *the Castillo de la Zuda, Tortosa, now a parador.*
Above right: *a corner of the dining room of the parador at* Tortosa.

Right: *looking out over the swimming pool.*

Light and shade at a window inside the parador at Tortosa.

The city of Tortosa seen through a window of the parador.
The effect is like that of a glass mosaic, and could even be
taken for a reflection in the waters of the Ebro.

A ferry on the Ebro delta. The river links Tortosa with the sea.

The Ebro on its course through the heart of Tortosa and, in the foreground, the Gothic cathedral.

ALCAÑIZ

Seen from many miles away, Alcañiz appears to be nothing more than a bald, flat-topped stone hill, a spot of ocher in a sea of trees and greenery. Long before he could see the town stretched out at the foot of the hill, the traveler took in the castle. A sturdy curtain wall encircles the escarpment, surrounding the 18th-century Aragonese palace; it is square in plan and set with corner towers, the walls plain on the first level and pierced by a profusion of balconies on the second.

Leaving the town behind him, the traveler drove up the Pui-Pinos hill, taking a road that circles it three times before it reaches the summit, and parked on the wide esplanade at the top.

Before entering the castle, he looked out over the wide landscape, a fertile land that from this eagle's nest can be seen to consist of orchards, olive groves, uncultivated patches, woods, and rivers that sparkle under the pure blue sky. He was moved to think how many illustrious historical figures who had inhabited the castle would have been filled with the very same sense of abundance at the sight of that landscape: there had been the Tiger of El Maestrazgo, leader of the Carlist wars in the 19th century; Alfonso the Battler, who ordered the city to be founded and built the castle in 1126; the brothers Fruela and Pelayo, the first two *alcaides*; Ramon Berenguer IV, who recaptured the castle from the Moors; and the Knights of Calatrava, the Spanish branch of the Knights Templar, who established their Aragonese seat here in 1179.

In 1411 the castle entered the annals of history when, within its walls, the Compromise of Caspe was signed. Charles V, that indefatigable traveler, also stayed there.

The traveler, taking comfort from such heroic thoughts, entered the parador and, having taken a room, walked across the tree-planted courtyard to visit the oldest parts of the castle, the great keep built by the Knights of Calatrava and the original Gothic cloister. For all that the keep is sturdy outside, inside it is homely and welcoming. On the first floor the visitor will find walls decorated with fine 14th-century frescoes; the bustle that once filled the castle is suddenly brought to life in all its detail in strong bright colors: here is a troubadour, there a dauphin, a cockerel, a knight, a fox, a man of letters ... and an enigmatic figure, a king who appears in three portraits that feature the same motto: *Regnabo, regno y regnavit.*

The visitor climbed a steep staircase to the second floor of the tower and looked out of the mullioned window, protected by a broad pointed shade that lets in a shaft of light. From here he let his gaze take in everything before him, from the red and

ALCAÑIZ

The parador of Alcañiz stands in the castle that Alfonso II gave to the Knights of Calatrava in 1179 so that they might build one of their monastery-fortresses there. It has an elegant keep with Gothic paintings, and a fine church with a tomb by the sculptor Damiá Forment. In 1728 Prince Philip, son of Philip V, remodeled the castle to make it more comfortable adding, among other features, a beautiful Baroque salon.

The parador at Alcañiz.

Within the castle walls stands a Romanesque church that contains the Plateresque tomb of Juan de Lamuza,
comendador and viceroy of Aragon, by the sculptor Damià Forment.

gray roofs of Alcañiz, so distant that all that he could hear of the town was a faint hum, to the Guadalupe plain, with its orderly fields and groves; the hazy blues in the far distance might either have been the skyline or the misty horizon of the Mediterranean.

With this panorama still imprinted on his mind's eye, the visitor entered the castle's church, a Romanesque building that contains a unique work of art, the tomb of Juan de Lanuza, *comendador* and viceroy of Aragon. This fine piece, sculpted in alabaster by Damià Forment in 1537, is an example of the Plateresque style. The tomb was once flanked by allegories of Fortitude and Temperance; for security reasons these are now kept in the town hall.

The traveler, whose appetite is always whetted by the presence of history, lunched on roast lamb washed down with Cariñena wine, strong and honorable as the land that produces it. For dessert he was unable to resist the *tetas de Santa Agueda* (St Agueda's breasts), a local specialty which proved as delicious as he had anticipated.

That afternoon the traveler took a stroll round the city, taking a particular interest in the 18th-century collegiate church and the 16th-century town hall, of which he had heard so much. The church is a major example of Baroque sculpture, both in its stone altarpiece and in its great ornate façade. The town hall is a sober three-story civic building, its serenity leavened by the pediment and the city's coat of arms on the facade.

Here in Alcañiz, as evening came, the traveler spotted flocks of jackdaws and swallows on their way south. "Like them," he thought, "it is time I ceased my wanderings and headed home." The next morning the sky was overcast and, his heart and his head packed full of memories, he set off northward, from whence he had come, firmly resolved to return one day to the fine places he had visited and the equally fine places he still had to see. For, as the sage once said, short is man's sojourn on earth, and only those endowed with curiosity for landscapes, people, and books may extend their lives at the expense of time, that great despot who wounds us every day and kills us on the last.

Opposite page: *three views of the parador at Alcañiz.*

A view of Alcañiz Cathedral from the parador.

Following pages: *St George's Day festivities in Alcañiz.*

*T*his map will be helpful to the reader who, like the imaginary traveler in the preceding pages, plans to set off on a fascinating journey, taking in the 29 historic paradors of Spain that have been described. Anyone who makes this journey will be rewarded with a wealth of sights, sensations, and impressions.

A suitable point of departure might well be Hondarribia. Running parallel to the Cantabrian coast, the route crosses Navarre and León, finally reaching Galicia. It then traverses Zamora and Salamanca, and penetrates Extremadura. This route leads from north to south, from the fresh waters of Galician rivers to the scorching sun of Andalusia, and northward again, from Castilla-La Mancha and Aragon, toward Catalonia and the waters of the Ebro.

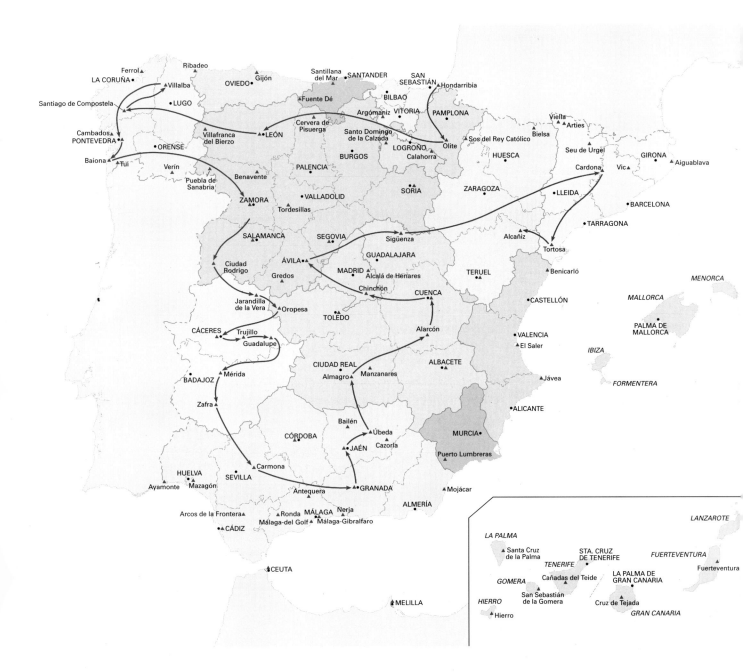

Ferrol
LA CORUÑA
Villalba
Ribadeo
OVIEDO Gijón
Santillana del Mar
SANTANDER
SAN SEBASTIÁN
Hondarribia
Santiago de Compostela
LUGO
Fuente Dé
BILBAO
Argómaniz VITORIA
PAMPLONA
Viella
Arties
Cambados
PONTEVEDRA
Villafranca del Bierzo
LEÓN
Cervera de Pisuerga
Santo Domingo de la Calzada
LOGROÑO
Calahorra
Olite
Sos del Rey Católico
HUESCA
Bielsa
Seu de Urgel
Baiona
Tui
Verín
Benavente
PALENCIA
BURGOS
Cardona
Vic
GIRONA
Aiguablava
ORENSE
Puebla de Sanabria
ZAMORA
Tordesillas
VALLADOLID
SORIA
ZARAGOZA
LLEIDA
BARCELONA
TARRAGONA
SALAMANCA
SEGOVIA
Sigüenza
Alcañiz
Tortosa
Ciudad Rodrigo
ÁVILA
GUADALAJARA
TERUEL
Benicarló
MENORCA
Gredos
MADRID
Alcalá de Henares
Jarandilla de la Vera
Chinchón
CUENCA
CASTELLÓN
MALLORCA
Oropesa
TOLEDO
Alarcón
VALENCIA
El Saler
PALMA DE MALLORCA
CÁCERES
Trujillo
Guadalupe
IBIZA
Mérida
CIUDAD REAL
Almagro
Manzanares
ALBACETE
Jávea
FORMENTERA
BADAJOZ
Bailén
Úbeda
Cazorla
MURCIA
ALICANTE
Zafra
CÓRDOBA
JAÉN
Puerto Lumbreras
Carmona
HUELVA
SEVILLA
Antequera
GRANADA
Mojácar
ALMERÍA
Ayamonte
Mazagón
Arcos de la Frontera
Ronda
MÁLAGA
Nerja
LANZAROTE
Málaga-del Golf
Málaga-Gibralfaro
CÁDIZ
LA PALMA
Santa Cruz de la Palma
STA. CRUZ DE TENERIFE
FUERTEVENTURA
CEUTA
TENERIFE
Cañadas del Teide
LA PALMA DE GRAN CANARIA
Fuerteventura
GOMERA
San Sebastián de la Gomera
Cruz de Tejada
MELILLA
HIERRO
Hierro
GRAN CANARIA

DIRECTORY OF PARADORS

Name:
Parador de Aiguablava

Address:
Platja d'Aiguablava, 17255 Bagur (Girona)

Description:
A modern purpose-built parador discreetly located in an area of coves
and pine woods. Ideal for sports and relaxation.

Name:
Parador de Alarcón

Address:
Avenida Amigos de los Castillos, 3, 16213 Alarcón (Cuenca)

Description:
A medieval fortress on the plains of La Mancha-Levante. Ideally located for
visiting interesting local churches and other monuments in the area.

Name:
Parador de Albacete

Address:
Carretera Nacional 301, Km 251, 02000 Albacete

Description:
Estate located in the heart of La Mancha, recommended for its peaceful
surroundings and relaxing atmosphere. Excellent cuisine.

Name:
Hostería de Alcalá de Henares

Address:
Colegios, 3, 28801 Alcalá de Henares (Madrid)

Description:
Formerly the Colegio Menor de San Jerónimo. An important historical complex,
within easy reach of Madrid.

Name:
Parador de Alcañiz

Address:
Castillo Calatravos, 44600 Alcañiz (Teruel)

Description:
Medieval castle-monastery of the Order of Calatrava set in a natural enclave of the Sierra de Maestrazgo, where excursions and sporting activities are organized. An interesting range of Gothic, Plateresque, and Baroque architecture.

Name:
Parador de Almagro

Address:
Ronda San Francisco, 31, 13270 Almagro (Ciudad Real)

Description:
A medieval monastery from which the visitor may conveniently explore the town and its natural surroundings, notably the Tablas de Daimiel. In July the Festival Internacional de Teátro Clásico takes place in the Corral de Comedias.

Name:
Parador de Antequera

Address:
Paseo García del Olmo, 29200 Antequera (Málaga)

Description:
A modern building with shady, refreshing gardens. Set in fertile lowlands, close to all major Andalusian capitals. Spacious, well-lit interiors.

Name:
Parador de Arcos de la Frontera

Address:
Plaza del Cabildo, 11630 Arcos de la Frontera (Cádiz)

Description:
A parador built in the local style, with typically Andalusian tilework and wrought ironwork. Located on the banks of the Guadalete, near Jerez de la Frontera, with views over the plain and the old center of Arcos. An ideal starting point for the itinerary to the Pueblos Blancos.

Name:
Parador de Argómaniz

Address:
Carretera N-1, km 363, 01192 Argómaniz (Álava)

Description:
Renaissance palace on Álava plain, within easy reach of Argómaniz and the Sierra de Gorbea. The rooms are furnished in a rustic style.

Name:
Parador de Artíes

Address:
Carretera Baqueira Beret, 25599 Artíes (Lleida)

Description:
Parador that offers a warm welcome in the heart of the Catalan Pyrenees, surrounded by unspoilt forest.

Name:
Parador de Ávila

Address:
Marqués de Canales de Chozas, 2, 05001 Ávila

Description:
Palace that nestles beneath the city walls. It has an intimate atmosphere, granite and adobe floors, and rooms with canopied beds.

Name:
Parador de Ayamonte

Address:
El Castillito, 21400 Ayamonte (Huelva)

Description:
A comfortable, modern parador set apart from the town. The cuisine includes Ayamonte-style fish and seafood.

Name:
Parador de Baiona

Address:
36300 Baiona (Pontevedra)

Description:
A medieval fortress with the elegance of an ancestral home. Panoramic views over the Atlantic.

Name:
Parador de Benavente

Address:
Plaza Ramón y Cajal, 49600 Benavente (Zamora)

Description:
Renaissance castle located in the old part of the walled city. The interior, with tapestries, wrought iron and Múdejar ceilings, has a robust appearance. Conveniently located for excursions to the Romanesque churches of Zamora.

Name:
Parador de Benicarló

Address:
Avenida Papa Luna, 5, 12580 Benicarló (Castellón)

Description:
A modern establishment with rooms overlooking the warm Mediterranean waters of the Costa del Azahar. Surrounded by gardens with palm trees. Excellent facilities, including swimming pool, tennis courts, and barbecue.

Name:
Parador de Bielsa

Address:
Valle de la Pineta, 22350 Bielsa (Huesca)

Description:
A modern building set in the heart of the Pyrenees. A haven of peace and tranquility, with pure air and clear streams, and Romanesque churches in the vicinity.

Name:
Parador de Cáceres

Address:
Calle Ancha, 6, 10003 Cáceres

Description:
A palace with Moorish origins and Gothic, Renaissance, and Baroque elements, located in the heart of the old town and blending sympathetically with surrounding towers, churches, and palaces.

Name:
Parador Hotel Atlántico. Cádiz

Address:
Avenida Duque de Nájera, 9, 11002 Cádiz

Description:
A modern purpose-built complex with views over the sea and Cádiz Bay. Large rooms and public areas suitable for a wide range of functions.

Name:
Parador de Calahorra

Address:
Paseo Mercadal, 26500 Calahorra (La Rioja)

Description:
A modern building overlooking the Valle de Cidacos and the banks of the Ebro, and blending sympathetically with this old Roman city with its great cathedral. Excellent Rioja cuisine.

Name:
Parador de Cambados

Address:
Paseo Calzada, 36630 Cambados (Pontevedra)

Description:
An old Galician Baroque pazo overlooking the green countryside through which flows the Baixas river. The pinewoods and beaches that line the Galician coast make this a particularly pleasant spot in summer. It is also within easy reach of the island of La Toxa.

Name:
Parador de Cañadas del Teide

Address:
Las Cañadas del Teide, 38300 La Orotava (Tenerife)

Description:
A chalet set high in the mountains, over 6500 feet above sea level. All the rooms have balconies commanding views of the peaks of El Teide, La Caldera, and La Montaña Blanca. It is the only building in El Teide national park. Typical Canary Islands cuisine.

Name:
Parador de Cardona

Address:
08261 Cardona (Barcelona)

Description:
A castle, with a keep and a Romanesque church within its walls, that towers majestically over the city of Cardona. The building itself and the decoration of the rooms take the visitor back to the High Middle Ages.

Name:
Parador de Carmona

Address:
Alcázar, 41410 Carmona (Sevilla)

Description:
A Moorish fortress located on the plain of the Carbones river. The décor, with classic Seville tilework and ironwork and a fine collection of antique tapestries and furniture, make this a particularly attractive parador.

Name:
Parador de Cazorla

Address:
Sierra de Cazorla, 23470 Cazorla (Jaén)

Description:
A building located at the heart of the Sierra de Cazorla, surrounded by extensive pine forests. The décor is that of a traditional Andalusian country house.

Name:
Parador de Cervera de Pisuerga

Address:
Carretera de Resova, km 2,5, 34840 Cervera de Pisuerga (Palencia)

Description:
A modern building, tastefully and elegantly decorated. Set in a splendid landscape, with views of the Picos de Europa and Ruesga lake.

Name:
Parador Hotel La Muralla

Address:
Plaza Ntra. Sra. de África, 15, 11701 Ceuta

Description:
A modern building located next to the royal walls in the heart of Ceuta. The original vaulting has been used for the ceilings of the rooms. Panoramic views over the sea.

Name:
Parador de Ciudad Rodrigo

Address:
Plaza Castillo, 1, 37500 Ciudad Rodrigo (Salalmanca)

Description:
A 16th-century castle located on the plain of the Agueda river. The keep can be seen for miles around. Within, the stone-arched public lounge is particularly attractive. An ideal place from which to explore Ciudad Rodrigo.

Name:
Parador de Córdoba

Address:
Avenida de la Arruzafa, 14012 Córdoba

Description:
This modern building stands on the site of the summer palace of Abd al-Rahman III, in the Cordoban sierra. It has attractive gardens, and is an ideal refuge from the heat of Córdoba in summer.

Name:
Hostería de Cruz de Tejeda

Address:
35328 Cruz de Tejeda, Isla de Gran Canaria (Las Palmas)

Description:
A typical Canary Islands manor house set in craggy landscape. Here the visitor can enjoy unspoilt views and the gentle climate of the Canary Islands.

Name:
Parador de Cuenca

Address:
Paseo de la Hoz del Huécar, 16001 Cuenca

Description:
A 16th-century monastery perched on the edge of a precipice in the city of Cuenca. The cloister and the former chapel, now the cafeteria, are two features of the parador that invite relaxation.

Name:
Parador de Chinchón

Address:
Avenida Generalísimo, 1, 28370 Chinchón (Madrid)

Description:
A former 17th-century convent located in the center of Chinchón, a town typical of the province of Madrid. It is next to the Paza Mayor, a fine example of vernacular architecture. The cloister has been converted into a cafeteria.

Name:
Parador de Ferrol

Address:
Calle Almirante Fernández Martín, 14401 Ferrol (La Coruña)

Description:
This building, an example of regional architecture, has a seafaring atmosphere in keeping with its location in a Galician port. The décor of the rooms, public areas and main staircase has a nautical theme. Impressive views of the port.

Name:
Parador de Fuente Dé

Address:
Fuente Dé, 39588 Fuente Dé (Cantabria)

Description:
A modern mountain retreat at the foot of the Picos de Europa with a typically mountain-style decor. A cable car takes visitor up to the Aliva, a high viewpoint. Many outdoor activities are organized.

Name:
Parador de Fuerteventura

Address:
Isla de Fuerteventura, Playa Blanca, 4535610 Fuerteventura (Las Palmas)

Description:
A colonial-style building surrounded by palms and located next to Playa Blanca, with views of the island's volcanic landscape.

Name:
Parador de Gijón

Address:
Parque Isabel la Católica, 33203 Gijón (Asturias)

Description:
The parador stands on the site of an old watermill. Set in an urban park, where peace and quiet are assured. Near to San Lorenzo beach and the marine district of Cimadevilla.

Name:
Parador de la Gomera

Address:
38800 San Sebastián de la Gomera, Isla de La Gomera (Santa Cruz de Tenerife)

Description:
This parador, built in a style characteristic of the Canary Islands, is an excellent base from which to explore Tenerife's beautiful landscapes. The interior has a nautical theme, recalling the great seafaring days of Christopher Columbus.

Name:
Parador de Granada

Address:
Real de la Alhambra, 18009 Granada

Description:
A 15th-century convent located next to the gardens of the Alhambra. The interior combines Moorish and Christian décor. The Albaicín and Generalife can be viewed from the balconies.

Name:
Parador de Gredos

Address:
Carretera Barraco de Béjar, km 43, 05132 Gredos (Ávila)

Description:
A modern stone-built parador located in the heart of the Gredos mountains, one of the most beautiful natural environments in Spain, with clear rivers, rugged rocks, and pine woods.

Name:
Parador de Guadalupe

Address:
Calle Marqués de la Romana, 10, 10140 Guadalupe (Cáceres)

Description:
Originally a 15th-century monastic hospital located in the historic city of Guadalupe, a World Heritage Site.

Name:
Parador de Hierro

Address:
Las Playas, 38900 El Hierro (Santa Cruz de Tenerife)

Description:
A modern parador which, nestling at the foot of Tenerife's volcanic landscape, is located right on the edge of the Atlantic Ocean.

Name:
Parador de Hondarribia

Address:
Plaza de Armas, 14, 20280 Hondarribia (Guipúzcoa)

Description:
The parador is located in a fine 10th-century fortified palace, which has survived virtually intact. The rooms look onto the sea and over to France.

Name:
Parador de Jaén

Address:
Castillo de Santa Catalina, 23001 Jaén

Description:
The parador is located in a medieval castle that stands on the Cerro de Santa Cantalina. Magnificent panoramic view of the city.

Name:
Parador de Jarandilla de la Vera

Address:
Avenida García Prieto, 1, 10450 Jarandilla de la Vera (Cáceres)

Description:
A fortified palace, once the residence of Charles V, with a great deal of regal charm. Located in the center of the Vergel de la Vera and El Tietár, in a landscape of oak and chestnut woods and deep gorges.

Name:
Parador de Jávea

Address:
Avenida del Mediterráneo, 7, 03730 Jávea (Alicante)

Description:
A modern establishment located at the northern end of the Costa Blanca and bathed by warm Mediterranean waters. Noted for its surrounding palm groves.

Name:
Parador Hostal San Marcos

Address:
Plaza San Marcos, 7, 24001 León

Description:
A former 16th-century monastery of the Order of Santiago, which functioned as a hospital. The exterior constitutes an important example of the Plateresque style.

Name:
Parador de Málaga-Gibralfaro

Address:
Castillo de Gibralfaro, 29016 Málaga

Description:
Located on Mount Gibralfaro, opposite the Alcazaba, and commanding views of the city and the bay. Well equipped for a wide range of sports, including golf and tennis.

Name:
Parador de Málaga-del Golf

Address:
Apartado de correos 324, 29080 Málaga

Description:
A building in the style of an Andalusian country house, opening onto extensive golf courses. Views of the sea and the Costa del Sol add to the parador's attractions.

Name:
Parador de Manzanares

Address:
Autovía de Andalucía, km 174, 13200 Manzanares (Ciudad Real)

Description:
A modern, La Mancha-style parador located between the Parque Natural de las Lagunas de Ruidera and the Tablas de Daimiel. The gardens, trees, and plants that surround the building create a green oasis in the Meseta.

Name:
Parador de Mazagón

Address:
Playa de Mazagón, 21130 Mazagón (Huelva)

Description:
Located in the Parque Natural de Doñana, this modern parador faces onto the beach and out over the sea. An ideal spot for the enjoyment of both the countryside and sea.

Name:
Parador de Melilla

Address:
Avenida Cándido Lobera, 29801 Melilla

Description:
This modern parador stands on a hill commanding a view of the walled city. It is flanked by long beaches bathed by the North African sun.

Name:
Parador de Mérida

Address:
Plaza de la Constitución, 3, 06800 Mérida (Badajoz)

Description:
An 18th-century convent in which many original features are preserved.
The ambience is in keeping with the cultural heritage of Mérida.

Name:
Parador de Mojácar

Address:
Playa de Mojácar, 04638 Mojácar (Almería)

Description:
This modern parador is located just above the beaches of Mojácar, where the best of Spain's climate can be enjoyed.

Name:
Parador de Nerja

Address:
Calle Almuñecar, 8, 29780 Nerja (Málaga)

Description:
This parador is located right on the beach. With its modern facilities and comfortable rooms, it is well suited to Spain's most cosmopolitan coastal resort.

Name:
Parador de Olite

Address:
Plaza Teobaldos, 2, 31390 Olite (Navarra)

Description:
A 15th-century castle, declared a national monument, which through its furnishings, stained-glass windows, and architectural features, preserves a medieval character.

Name:
Parador de Oropesa

Address:
Plaza Palacio, 1, 45560 Oropesa (Toledo)

Description:
A 14th-century fortified palace with magnificent views of the Gredos mountains. Original architectural features and medieval furniture contribute to an authentic atmosphere.

Name:
Parador de Pontevedra

Address:
Calle Barón, 19, 36002 Pontevedra

Description:
A 16th-century Renaissance palace located in the center of this beautiful Galician city. An ideal base from which to explore the secluded coves and beaches nearby.

Name:
Parador de Puebla de Sanabria

Address:
Carretera Lago, 18, 49300 Puebla de Sanabria (Zamora)

Description:
This modern parador is located on the edge of Europe's largest glacial lake. An ideal base for excursions into the beautiful surrounding countryside. Views of the historic town of Puebla de Sanabria.

Name:
Parador de Puerto Lumbreras

Address:
Avenida Juan Carlos I, 77, 30890 Puerto Lumbreras (Murcia)

Description:
This modern parador is a haven of rest and relaxation. It is a convenient base from which to explore the beauty of the Murcia region.

Name:
Parador de Ribadeo

Address:
Calle Amador Fernández, 7, 27700 Ribadeo (Lugo)

Description:
A Galician mansion located on the Eo estuary, with views of the Lugo coastline. The simple elegance of the house is typical of the coastal architecture of the area.

Name:
Parador de Ronda

Address:
Plaza de España, 29400 Ronda (Málaga)

Description:
Located in what was once a civic building. While the original façade has been preserved, the interior has been modernized. It overlooks the gorge of the Tagus.

Name:
Parador de Salamanca

Address:
Calle Teso de la Feria, 2, 37008 Salamanca

Description:
This spacious, comfortable establishment stands on the banks of the Tormes river. Set on a hillside, with views of the cathedral.

Name:
Parador de Saler

Address:
Avenida de los Pinares, 151, 46012 El Saler (Valencia)

Description:
This modern parador is equipped with a world-class golf course as well as facilities and services that make it ideal for family holidays.

Name:
Parador de Santa Cruz de La Palma

Address:
Avenida Marítima, 38700 Santa Cruz de La Palma, Isla de La Palma (Santa Cruz de Tenerife)

Description:
A typical Canary Islands building with wooden balconies that look out over the city. A convenient base from which to explore the beauties of the island.

Name:
Parador Hostal de los Reyes Católicos

Address:
Plaza do Obradoiro, 1, 15705 Santiago de Compostela (La Coruña)

Description:
This historic building was originally a hostel for pilgrims founded by the Catholic Kings in the 15th century. Today it is one of the finest and most luxurious paradors, distinguished not only because of its architectural importance but on account of its location, next to the cathedral.

Name:
Parador de Santillana del Mar

Address:
Plaza Ramón Pelayo, 11, 39330 Santillana del Mar (Cantabria)

Description:
This is an ancestral home, built in a sober and robust style, located in a town that has been declared a national monument.

Name:
Parador de Santo Domingo de la Calzada

Address:
Plaza del Santo, 3, 26250 Santo Domingo de la Calzada (La Rioja)

Description:
This parador is located in a building whose origins, as a hostel, go back to the 12th century. It stands next to the cathedral. Remarkable among its architectural features are its great arcaded halls. The restaurant specializes in the local Riojan cuisine.

Name:
Parador de Segovia

Address:
Carretera de Valladolid, 40003 Segovia

Description:
This modern parador, fully equipped for comfort and relaxation, commands a fine view of the city of Segovia, which has been declared a World Heritage Site. It is also a useful base for exploring the local countryside.

Name:
Parador de Seo de Urgell

Address:
Calle Sant Domenec, 6, 25700 Seo de Urgell (Lleida)

Description:
A modern parador located in a converted convent. The cloister is attractively covered in climbing plants. Views of the nearby cathedral and Segre river.

Name:
Parador de Sigüenza

Address:
Plaza del Castillo, 19250 Sigüenza (Guadalajara)

Description:
A 12th-century medieval castle built on the site of Moorish alcazaba, ideal for exploring an unspoilt medieval town. The parador is simply decked out with the furnishings of the Spanish Middle Ages.

Name:
Parador de Soria

Address:
Parque del Castillo, 42005 Soria

Description:
A parador with modern facilities located in unspoilt countryside. Views over the city and Duero river.

Name:
Parador de Sos del Rey Católico

Address:
Calle Arq. Sainz de Vicuña, ,1, 50680 Sos del Rey Católico (Zaragoza)

Description:
This parador, in the style of an Aragonese mansion, overlooks the historic medieval town of Sos del Rey Católico. Views of the Pyrenean foothills.

Name:
Parador de Teruel

Address:
Carretera Sagunto-Burgos, 44080 Teruel

Description:
A small palace in the local Mudéjar style, located on the outskirts of the city. Marble, tilework, horseshoe arches and other Moorish elements make for an attractive décor.

Name:
Parador de Toledo

Address:
Cerro del Emperador, 45002 Toledo

Description:
A parador with a décor of tiles, wood, brick, and stone, located on the banks of the Tagus. It commands panoramic view of the city, whose synagogues, cathedral, and citadel are well worth a visit.

Name:
Parador de Tordesillas

Address:
Carretera de Salamanca, 5, 47100 Tordesillas (Valladolid)

Description:
A Castilian ancestral home located near a beautiful pine wood. This Castilian city is of great historical renown and its parador offers guests a haven of peace and tranquility in an unusually attractive setting.

Name:
Parador de Tortosa

Address:
Castillo de la Zuda, 43500 Tortosa (Tarragona)

Description:
A 10th-century fortified palace located on the Ebro delta at the foot of the Beceite mountains. It stands above the city, and contains many great artistic treasures dating from the time of Abd ar-Rahman III.

Name:
Parador de Trujillo

Address:
Calle Santa Beatriz de Silva, 1, 10200 Trujillo (Cáceres)

Description:
An atmosphere of peace and tranquility pervades this parador, located in a 16th-century converted convent. The town is the birthplace of several notable Spanish seafarers.

Name:
Parador de Tui

Address:
Avenida de Portugal, 36700 Tui (Pontevedra)

Description:
This parador, in a converted Galician pazo (country house), is located just to the north of the Portuguese coastline. The stonework and chestnut timbers give it a typically Galician character.

Name:
Parador de Úbeda

Address:
Plaza de Vázquez Molina, 23400 Úbeda (Jaén)

Description:
A 16th-century Renaissance palace located in an attractive city. Set in the main square, it is a central point of departure for the visitor wanting to explore Úbeda.

Name:
Parador de Verín

Address:
32600 Verín (Orense)

Description:
A Galician country house with a crenelated keep commanding a fine view of the town.

Name:
Parador de Vic

Address:
Paraje el Bac de Sau, 08500 Vic (Barcelona)

Description:
A parador with the air of a traditional Catalan masía. Located on the edge of the Sau reservoir, it will appeal to nature-lovers and is ideal for watersports.

Name:
Parador de Viella

Address:
Carretera del Tunel, 25530 Viella (Lleida)

Description:
This modern mountain parador is located in the enchanting Vall d'Aran. An ideal base for hikers and skiers.

Name:
Parador de Villafranca del Bierzo

Address:
Avenida de Calvo Sotelo, 24500 Villafranca del Bierzo (León)

Description:
A traditional mansion in this major Leonese town, which was once a stopping place for pilgrims on the road to Santiago. The parador is decorated in the traditional Castilian style.

Name:
Parador de Villalba

Address:
Calle San Valeriano Valdesuso, 27800 Villalba (Lugo)

Description:
A strong historical atmosphere, redolent of medieval Galicia, pervades this impressive keep, now converted into a parador.

Name:
Parador de Zafra

Address:
Plaza Corazón de María, 7, 06300 Zafra (Badajoz)

Description:
The walls of this 15th-century fortified palace make it an attractive retreat. The city of Zafra offers much of interest and is set in the typical landscape of Extremadura.

Name:
Parador de Zamora

Address:
Plaza de Viriato, 5, 49001 Zamora

Description:
A 15th-century Renaissance palace located in the historic heart of this great Castilian city. Tapestries, suits of armor, and canopied beds enhance the parador's historical atmosphere.